African Land Rights Systems

Aquiline Tarimo

Langaa Research & Publishing CIG
Mankon, Bamenda

Publisher:
Langaa RPCIG
Langaa Research & Publishing Common Initiative Group
P.O. Box 902 Mankon
Bamenda
North West Region
Cameroon
Langaagrp@gmail.com
www.langaa-rpcig.net

Distributed in and outside N. America by African Books Collective
orders@africanbookscollective.com
www.africanbookcollective.com

ISBN: 9956-792-60-8

Table of Contents

Acknowledgments

The issue of land rights is apparently neglected in African studies on ethics, culture, and religion. The reason is that land is understood as a matter to be exploited to satisfy human needs. Studies on land, from the perspective of the existing literature, have been left to geographers, lawyers, historians, and sociologists who present land-related issues in terms of reports that lack critical analyses, hermeneutical insights, ethical questions, and transformative suggestions. The concept of land, seemingly, comes to the ethical discourse from the sidelines, not straightforwardly in the manner we expect because of its importance.

This book is enriched by interviews I had with people affected by land-related clashes, evictions, and civil wars from Kenya, Tanzania, Burundi, Rwanda, Ethiopia, and Sudan. Among those I interviewed include victims of eviction from the slums and refugees from the camps of Kakuma in Kenya, Rhino Camp in Uganda, and Mishamo Resettlement Scheme in Kigoma, Tanzania. I also interviewed scholars, activists, and officials working in the department of migration attempting to address problems accompanying cross-border migration and intra-state displacement. I have also interviewed people working in research centers, including Jesuit Hakimani Center in Nairobi, Kenya and reporters of the events of land-related conflicts in Mtwara and Arusha, Tanzania. Graduate theses that I have supervised at the Institute of Peace Studies and International Relations, Hekima College, Nairobi, Kenya and elsewhere, for many years, have also helped me to be familiar with African land rights systems, a perspective that I explore in this book. The

v

people I interviewed from many parts of Africa on this subject make the ideas that I present in this book contextual and timely.

The study, nonetheless, does not intend to present a report of these experiences. It does not even confine itself within the parameters of philosophy, history, or theology. Its scope cuts across many disciplines of study with an intention of producing effective methodologies of addressing problems related to land rights systems. My hope is that this approach will contribute to a better understanding of the conditions surrounding land disputes. It is my hope that this book will serve as a resource for those who are involved in the effort of resolving land disputes, resettlement, and integration. I am convinced that questions raised will produce a renewed motivation to examine African land rights systems.

Many people deserve appreciation for their assistance in the course of writing this book. I owe a debt of gratitude to Peter Clark, S.J., and Joseph Godfrey, S.J., from the Jesuit Community at Saint Joseph's University, Pennsylvania. I am grateful to the Jesuit Community as a whole for providing me a supportive environment for research. On this account I am grateful to Brendan Lally, S.J., Rector of the Jesuit Community, and Michael Hricko, S.J., the Administrator of the same Jesuit Community. They granted me facility, time, and care I needed to undertake an academic writing. The encouragement and companionship that came from my Jesuit colleagues from other parts of the United States of America, especially from Paul Fitzgerald, S.J., at Fairfield University and William O'Neill, S.J., at Santa Clara University, also proved to be helpful.

I am also grateful to Saint Joseph's University for granting me Donald MacLean Chair for one academic year. The three public lectures I presented at the university reshaped my ideas on land rights. The academic staff and students helped me to shape certain aspects of my research and writing. The library personnel helped me to get the books that I could not get in African libraries. I am sincerely grateful to them.

Finally, many thanks go to those who wrote the books and articles that I cited. To end the vote of thanksgiving I cannot forget those who read the manuscript with a view to improve my contribution. On this account I remember Prof. James Redington, S.J., Dr. Festo Mkenda, S.J., Dr. Thaddeus C. Raezknoski, Joan Delvin, and Donald Ward, S.J. Those that I cannot mention here I am also grateful to their assistance.

Introduction

Land is a sensitive subject because it is one of the most valuable resources for survival. It provides food, water, energy, and other benefits to meet the needs of human beings. It is a resource from which many people make a living. Despite the importance of land, seemingly, most of the challenging questions about distribution, ownership, and management have not yet received adequate attention.

At the moment there is a growing literature on land-related disputes. But most of it is bereft of ethical analyses, conclusions, and recommendations. There is no attempt to establish the link between cause and effect with an intention to unveil the background of the problem and what could be done to produce a long-term solution. Many approaches concentrate on reporting what is happening without giving reasons underlying the root causes.[1] Migrants, refugees, and internally-displaced persons "articulating claims around land rights are largely ignored as are the land rights programs of urban-based human rights organizations."[2] A reform of the existing land rights systems is required because they cannot guarantee security for vulnerable individuals, groups, and communities.

There are few studies on land rights that have thoroughly examined the relationship between land, market, and morality.[3] A critical reflection on this aspect could help us to know the extent to which the trend of land-grabbing has contributed toward the depletion of the farmland, landlessness, inequality, migration, and conflict. Meanwhile we need studies that can generate analyses, conclusions, and recommendations to support the effort of protecting forests required for rain, public land for future development, and rights for the vulnerable communities.[4] These studies must also be able to present something more than unexamined empirical data, an approach that has saturated the existing land rights literature.

The issue of land rights is apparently neglected in African studies on ethics, culture, and religion. The reason is that land is understood as a matter to be exploited to satisfy human needs. Studies on land, from the perspective of the existing literature, have been left to geographers, historians, and sociologists who present land-related issues in terms of reports that lack critical analyses, hermeneutical insights, ethical questions, and transformative suggestions. The concept of land, seemingly, comes to the ethical discourse from the sidelines, not straightforwardly in the manner we expect because of its importance.

Comparative approaches are mostly focused on reports and statistics without any concern for the reasons underlying the events they report about that raise questions or suggest ways that can change the situation. Land rights discourse must necessarily include ontological and teleological dimensions. It is an issue that brings together ideas, feelings, experiences, and expectations. It concerns systems of culture, belief, and economics. It is about raising questions and exploring reasons underlying land disputes accompanied with conclusions and recommendations that could enrich land rights debate and policymaking procedure.

I agree with Jean-Philippe Platteau that "land ownership problems have become a source of the increasing inequality and food insecurity among the vulnerable sections of the rural population."[5] Even when the disputes have been resolved by the courts, "the bitterness lingers on in the minds of the litigants. The legal conflict may come to an end, but the real conflict lives on."[6] The increasing insecurity and conflict around the land question results from the lack of coordination among different land rights systems, namely, customary, private, and statutory. These differences enhance separate legislations that generate a barrier for initiatives intending to formulate a unified land law. In many African countries, observes Frank Byamugisha, "disputes related to land constitute a very high percentage of court cases. In Ghana, for example, fifty percent of all new civil cases lodged are related to land, while in Ethiopia, one-third to half of all cases within the formal judicial system are related to land."[7]

Access to land has a profound impact on people's ability to be self-sufficient. The historical background of the African continent shows that unlawful acquisition of land from traditional communities during the colonial period rendered many people landless, insecure, and vulnerable. Farmlands were arbitrarily taken from the indigenous people by colonial agents.[8] Repossessing stolen lands, as a motive of the independence struggle, was regarded as a guarantee of autonomy and self-determination to the people. Since then land has continued to dictate the rhythm of social relations. Others would argue that land is the locus of social relations. A number of African countries, including Kenya, Zimbabwe, and South Africa, to the present day, continue to struggle with unresolved land-related disputes that have become a source of insecurity, forced migration, and civil strife.[9]

Land ownership correlates to identity, belonging, community, and autonomy because it is connected to social relations stretched over a certain territory. Land disputes evolved through different historical periods: traditional, colonial, and post-colonial. Each period encountered different circumstances and difficulties. The existing land rights disputes culminate into these trends. The problem became intense during the period of European industrial revolution because the colonial regime acquired land from conquered territories for cultivation and mining.

Land, as the most important aspect in the history of African nationalism, "was the basis upon which the war for independence was waged."[10] The formation of the nation-states and social relations revolves around the land question. Land, to the present day, continues to be the most important subject for public debate because it occupies a privileged status in socio-economic organization, cultural traditions, and social relations.

In recent years, similarly, foreign investors have acquired huge chunks of land which add a complex dimension to the question of land distribution and ownership.[11] The land crisis has been intensified by the fact that countries dependent on food imports attempt to guarantee their food supply by adopting the approach of buying land in third world countries to grow their own food. Other countries are trying to replace the diminishing oil reserves by developing industries that can produce bio-fuel products. These trends have resulted in land-grabbing from small-scale farmers and public land reserves.[12] To this end, clearly, huge quantities of land upon which small-scale farmers grow food for local consumption are taken by multinational corporations organized to produce food for the international market. The system is progressively generating landlessness, inequality, and conflict. Looking at the current situation one could argue that land disputes are the root causes of the conflicts prevailing at the grassroots level.[13]

Analyses of the existing conflicts reveal profound connections between land distribution and civil unrest.[14] For example, the civil wars of Nigeria, Cote d'Ivoire, and Sudan revolved around the claims of territorial control and cultural identity. At the grassroots level, as witnessed in many countries, there is prolonged tension, mistrust, and conflict between agriculturalist communities and pastoralist communities characterized by fights over water, pasture, and farmland. Extreme inequality emanates from unjust distribution of land. Promises of land reform, made more than six decades ago, remain unfulfilled. These conditions underscore the existing sensitivity on the land rights question.

Peasantry is unreliable because it does not produce enough food. Weaknesses of peasantry include the lack of agricultural machinery, insecure land tenure, inadequate output, and environmental destruction. In certain areas, agricultural production is also limited because of the increase of population. And "when land acquires scarcity value, landholders begin to feel uncertain about the strength of their customary rights, and disputes over ownership of land, inheritance, and land boundaries tend to multiply."[15] Land disputes, with a threat to public order, are increasingly becoming common at the grassroots level.

One could argue that the difficulties accompanying the land question amount to the fact that the land issue is not a single problem requiring a single remedy. Rather, it is a culmination of issues related to the access toward resources, "distribution of power among citizens, and local systems of authority found in everyday struggles over land, which include claims, counter-claims, and the struggles for survival."[16] These problems are caused by population growth, extreme inequality, environmental destruction, and mismanagement, which involves land-grabbing by foreign agro-business companies. Land disputes are not caused by a single issue of contention. Rather, they derive from a condition that involves a whole series of issues among many others expressed in terms of acquisition and control of resources. Problems of administration, limited technological advancement, inequality, insecurity, and conflict are issues that relate to land. Such a situation justifies the argument that there cannot be a single remedy to land disputes.

African land disputes could be summed up in three categories. First, land dispute occurs when peasants and herders are competing for farmland, freshwater, and pasture. It occurs when there is a prolonged season of drought, population growth, or environmental degradation. This experience is common in Kenya, Uganda, Tanzania, and Mali. Second, land disputes flare up when refugees and internally-displaced persons return to their homeland only to find the land they left behind is occupied and claimed by other people. This is common for countries that have experienced civil wars such as Burundi, Uganda, Rwanda, and South Sudan. Third, foreign investors, in recent years, have been grabbing land for mining and agribusiness ventures. This situation has occurred in Madagascar, Mozambique, Ethiopia, and Tanzania. It is a situation that is fueling inter-communal conflict, eviction, and civil strife. Land disputes at the grassroots level are intensifying and becoming a widespread trend. It is reasonable to search for long-term remedies to the increasing land disputes instead of perceiving them as temporary and isolated events.

The aim of this study, from ethical, interdisciplinary, and African perspectives, is to unveil the root causes of the increasing land disputes. This presentation, being an evaluation, does not intend to present sociological data in terms of reports, statistics, or interviews drawn from a single context for empirical verification.[17] Many scholars, from sociological, political, and historical perspectives, have extensively presented these findings. What is missing in the existing literature on land disputes is an ethical-critical analysis, a void that this evaluation intends to fill.

The significance of this study lies in the effort of presenting a broad overview founded upon a critical analysis of the existing land-related literature. It is a perspective that attempts to consolidate the renewed interest in the evolving theories of land rights by raising questions that can help us to understand better the prevailing confusion pertaining to the land ownership systems, conflict between customary and statutory land rights systems, and the politics of land reform.

The methodology underlying the study provides a perspective that raises questions intended to identify areas of contention, dispute, and conflict. Its specificity lies in ethical provisions viewed from the perspective of land rights. The study, which could also be categorized as a critical assessment of the African land rights systems, is intended to be a resource for scholars, activists, and organizations seeking to resolve land disputes.

The study is organized into three chapters. The first chapter attempts to identify the root causes of land disputes by examining the relationship between land, identity, and self-determination. The claims of identity, belonging, and ownership have strongly emerged as conditions threatening to tear contemporary Africa apart. The paradoxical nature accompanying these claims makes the three variables paradigms of inclusion and exclusion. Observations, analyses, and conclusions resulting from the evaluation could help us to understand the connection between spirituality, anthropology, environment, privatization of land rights, and the politics of land reform. The second chapter examines the relationship between land, market, and morality. This extension becomes necessary because the meanings, values, and functions of land are often limited to the market value.

The third chapter demonstrates how the claims of land rights moderate the trends of migration, resettlement, and integration. Problems accompanying these trends are addressed by examining the impact of landlessness, the status of migrants and refugees, and the ambiguities of belonging and citizenship.

Notes

---

[1] Social sciences, due to the lack of adequate focus on hermeneutics, tend to concentrate on reporting events and statistics. Transformative conclusions and recommendations require more than that. Contemporary Africa needs analyses that can penetrate sociological reality in view of telling us what happened, what could happen in the future, and what must be done to change the situation. Our interest is in the future, not only in the historical events that represent the past.

[2] Jacqueline M. Klopp, "Pilfering the Public: The Problem of Land Grabbing in Contemporary Kenya," *Africa Today* 47, 1 (Winter 2000): 7-26, at 9.

[3] Among the few existing publications include Stein T. Holden et al., eds., *The Emergence of Land Markets in Africa: Impacts on Poverty, Equity, and Efficiency* (Washington, D.C.: Resources for the Future, 2009); Ambreena Manji, *The Politics of Land Reform in Africa: From Communal Tenure to Free Markets* (London: Zed Books, 2006); Bill Derman et al., eds., *Conflicts Over Land and Water in Africa* (London: James Currey Limited, 2007). The greater part of these publications is, however, a collection of empirical data. They present limited analyses, conclusions, and recommendations.

[4] Klopp, "Pilfering the Public: The Problem of Land Grabbing in Contemporary Kenya," 7.

[5] Jean-Philippe Platteau, *Land Reform and Structural Adjustment in Sub-Saharan Africa: Controversies and Guidelines* (Rome: Food and Agricultural Organization, Economic and Social Policy Department, 1992), 1.

[6] Smokin C. Wanjala, *Land Law and Disputes in Kenya* (Nairobi: Oxford University Press, 1990), ix-x.

[7] Frank F.K. Byamugisha, *Securing Africa's Land for Shared Prosperity: A Program to Scale-Up Reforms and Investments* (Washington, D.C.: World Bank, 2013), 20.

[8] For further elaboration see Gershon Feder and Raymond Noronha, "Land Rights Systems and Agricultural Development in Sub-Saharan Africa," *Research Observer* 2, 2 (July 1987): 143-169.

[9] Lucas Barasa, "Why Land is Main Cause of Conflict," *Daily Nation*, Kenya (May 23, 2013): 22. For analytical presentations, see Urmilla Bob, "Land-Related Conflicts in Sub-Saharan Africa," *African Journal of Conflict Resolution* 10, 2 (June 2010): 49-64; R.E. Downs and S.P. Reyna, eds., *Land and Society in Contemporary Africa* (Hanover: University Press of New England, 1988).

[10] The Ndungu Report, "Land Graft in Kenya," *Review of African Political Economy* 32, 103 (March 2005): 142-151, at 142.

[11] World Council of Churches, "Land and Spirituality in Africa," *http://www.wcc-coe.org/wccwhat/jpc/echoes-16-05.html* (Accessed December 20, 2012).

[12] For empirical evidence showing how land-grabbing has been growing quickly in recent years, see Sam Moyo, *African Land Question, Agrarian Transactions and the State: Contradictions of Neo-Liberal Land* Reform (Dakar: Sapes Books, 2008), 51-55; Jacqueline M. Klopp, "Pilfering the Public: The Problem of Land Grabbing in Kenya," *Africa Today* 47, 1 (March 1999): 7-26; Francois Houtart, *Agrofuels: Big Profits, Ruined Lives and Ecological Destruction* (Amsterdam: Pluto Press, 2010); Prosper B. Matondi et al., eds.,

Biofuels, Land Grabbing and Food Security in Africa (London: Zed Books Ltd, 2011); John A. Allan et al., *Handbook of Land and Water Grabs in Africa: Foreign Direct Investment and Water Security* (Oxford: Routledge, 2012); Lorenzo Cotula, *The Great African Land Grab* (London: Zed Books Limited, 2013); Ward Anseeuw and Chris Alden, eds., *The Struggle Over Land in Africa: Conflicts, Politics, and Change* (Cape Town: HSRC Press, 2010); Rose Mwalongo, "Kilombero Boiling with Land-Grabbing Disputes," *The Guardian, Tanzania* (July 11, 2013): 5.

[13] For verification about how land-grabbing has been growing to the extent of becoming a threat for development and state sovereignty, see Robin Palmer, "The Land Problems in Africa: The Second Scramble," *New People* 54 (June 2002): 13-22.

[14] Ward Anseeuw and Chris Alden, "Introduction," in Ward Anseeuw and Chris Alden, eds., *The Struggle Over Land in Africa: Conflicts, Politics, and Change* (Cape Town: Human Sciences Research Council, 2010), 1-15, at 1.

[15] Jean-Philippe Plateau, "Does Africa Need Land Reform?" in Camila Toulmin and Julian Quan, eds., *Evolving Land Rights, Policy and Tenure in Africa* (London: IIED, 2000), 51-96, at 54.

[16] Christian Lund, *Land Rights and Citizenship in Africa* (Uppsala: Nordiska Afrikainstitutet, 2011), 5.

[17] The scope of the evaluation is not limited to a case study from a single location because the challenge of land disputes is a widespread problem in contemporary Africa. Excessive focus on sociological data drawn from a single location could limit the scope of the evaluation altogether.

Chapter 1

Land, Identity, and Self-Determination

The decline of spirituality of the land that links human beings to the natural world has weakened the meaning of land. The reason is that market forces have taken over the responsibility of land management in which land is perceived as a matter to be exploited for economic interest. The situation has also been aggravated by the tendency of limiting land ownership to the privileged minority. The resulting consequences include land-related disputes and civil strife at the grassroots level.

The aim of this chapter is to identify the root causes of the increasing land-related disputes by examining the relationship between land, identity, and self-determination. The exploration begins with a claim that the meaning of land is attached to the religious and cultural dimensions that brings together the natural world and social relations. This platform is extended further by arguing that land is the foundation of claims of identity, belonging, and community. Given the importance of territorial integrity, the analysis extends these connections toward the claims of ownership, autonomy, and self-determination. The focus on privatization of the land rights, thereafter, advances an argument that mismanagement renders the connection between land ownership and social relations problematic. In search for methodologies of addressing the situation, the analysis concludes with an examination of the politics of land reform.

Religious and Cultural Dimensions of Land

It is difficult to give a straightforward definition of land because it has multiple meanings, values, and functions. This condition confirms that the meaning of land is tied to different dimensions of human experience. As a starting point, however, we can simply say that land is a natural resource that provides food, water, and energy to meet human needs.

Land is sometimes defined symbolically because it is attached to the sacred dimension. Mythologies describe the origin of the land as a divine gift entrusted to human beings. A number of religious and cultural narratives confirm this perception by asserting that a supernatural being created the earth and people. These narratives inhabit the mind of people as a part of the collective memory. Land is a collective reference because it forms the imagination required for building a community. Identification of the individuals, groups, and communities is formed around a concept of land. A community of human beings is defined using a paradigm of collective memories extended to a given territory as a part of its identity.[1] People are emotionally attached to the birthplace as a way of laying down a foundation for their identity.[2] Land forms a part of a conceptual framework that embodies the process of constructing identity as well as forming a platform underlying the claim of belonging. It upholds the definition of belonging to form a community.

Land, from the perspective of the Judeo-Christian biblical tradition, for example, is considered to be a gift infused with divine energy. According to God's plan we cannot use it in such a way that it only benefits the privileged; rather, it is entrusted to the community with moral obligations that entail just distribution and responsible use.[3] The biblical tradition

2

appears within the practice of land redistribution in every jubilee year with a special concern for those who are alienated from their land.[4] The jubilee year mandates the return of the land to its original owners.[5]

Private ownership is a form of stewardship exercised on behalf of the community. It is not a permanent ownership because it is conditioned by the needs of the community. The ethics of responsible stewardship challenge greed by appealing to the common good. Such a perspective expresses concern over the claim of collective needs by challenging the tendency of accumulation founded upon the ideology of privatization that concentrates land in the hands of a few people.

The biblical tradition reminds the people of Israel that "land must not be sold on a permanent basis because people do not own it; land belongs to God, and people are tenants who are allowed to make use of it."[6] The demand of responsible stewardship alluded here could be summed up in three ways: first, land is sacred and belongs to the community; second, people are stewards of the land entrusted to them; and third, land must be used in a way that generates moderate livelihood for all.

In African cosmologies, people perceive human beings as an integral part of the natural world.[7] The value of land is intrinsically connected to spiritual, ethical, and economic dimensions. The sacred dimension refers to the roles of the ancestors, spirits, and deities to regulate land use. We can also say that land is an embodiment of the divine.[8] Mountains and rivers, for example, provide sacred sites to offer prayers, rituals, and sacrifices. These features are regarded as centers of deities who guard the fertility of the land. It is for this reason that one could say the spiritual dimension connects people to the natural world.

Some cultural traditions and belief systems uphold that the earth is animated by divine presence that shapes the life of all created things. The sacred dimension of land requires communities to regulate human relations as a way of monitoring the way land is used. It provides a possibility to examine the interaction between material and non-material dimensions in the process of conceptualizing the value of land. Traditional communities remain attached to the value systems that connect people to the natural world. For Kikuyu people, writes Jomo Kenyatta, "land is sacred because it feeds the child for life and nurses the dead for eternity."[9] Confirmation of the sacred dimension of land is also evident when land is transferred from one person to another. People perceive land transfer as a sacred process. There would be a ceremony in the court of the elders to approve the transfer, showing that it is a spiritual process rather than a market transaction.[10] Traditions that maintain such a worldview reinforce the bond that exists between human beings and the natural world. People believe that the earth is animated by spirits and deities for the purpose of maintaining harmony and beauty.[11] This perception functions as a means of connecting people to the earth. The sacred dimension provides a framework that addresses complex moral questions.

This convergence of material and non-material dimensions forms a unified value of the land. Land is not a mere economic reality. It has spiritual and cultural attributes enshrined into it. This perspective provides an insight which confirms that the spiritual dimension provides a ground for the construction of identity. The meaning of land is embodied in value systems that operate in terms of traditions. This assertion refers to the connection between identity and community, which shows that land-grabbing does not only take away the livelihood of a given people, it also undermines religious and cultural traditions.

Traditional communities are tied to certain locations with which they establish spiritual and cultural relations. The spiritual dimension, it might be said, serves as a connection between spirit, land, and people.[12] Members of the community claim that ancestral land is inherited following the rationale of blood relations in trust for future generations. To this end, corporately considered, the tradition makes land a right upon which every member is entitled to own a piece.

The ethical and legal conceptualization of land ownership correlates to spiritual identity.[13] The Igbo people of Nigeria, for example, view land as a reality that has both spiritual and ethical implications because it is a resource that establishes a link between the physical world and human beings.[14] "Ancestral land impacts on people's identity, on the ways they are bound to the land and relate to their natural surroundings, as well as to fundamental feelings of connectedness with the social and cultural environment in its entirety."[15] The living members believe that land is entrusted to them as a religio-cultural heritage.[16]

There is an intrinsic connection between people, spirit, and land that sustains the livelihood of the community. The God-people-land relationship is a unified structure embedded within the formula of creation. Land is animated by the sacred dimension because "it belongs to spirits, deities, and ancestors."[17] The sacred dimension refers to the origin of created things, spiritual potency, and the divine energy that animate the earth to sustain life. It is from this understanding that the idea of selling land rights becomes unacceptable. The sacredness and value of land arise from the understanding that land is a reality that constitutes the claims of identity and belonging. The condition in which we live confines the meaning of land to the market value by ignoring the connection between material and non-material dimensions of human existence.

The function of land is to mediate spiritual awareness, cultural traditions, economic life, and social relations. If land "consists of material and non-material values, then it cannot be adequately valued in commercial terms alone."[18] The utilitarian approach limits the value of land to the material dimension, which stands as a determinant variable for its market value. In this case, money, being the measure of utility, becomes the measure of values possible to human beings. If a human being is an embodiment of the material and non-material values, then, a human being is the locus of all values. Focusing exclusively on the material dimension undermines the import of spirituality, morality, and culture to human life.

Traditional communities do not view land as a material entity only, but rather as a part of spiritual, ethical, and legal matrix that shapes social relations. They use the language of spirituality to identify the connection between land and people. Deities, as spiritual guardians, grant land to the people as a part of a broad spectrum of social relations, which include customs, beliefs, and norms. Some African mythologies uphold that human beings were created out of clay, thereby making the earth the origin of human beings.[19] The dominance of the market is increasingly generating a spiritual vacuum. The situation affects the way land is perceived and managed to the detriment of religio-cultural traditions.

Land is considered to be a spiritual and cultural heritage entrusted to the community, and it can only be transferred from one person to another following the affinity of blood relations. The sacredness of land refers to the argument that it is a life-giving reality, and without it we cannot relate human existence to the story of creation. The loss of moral accountability raises questions about spirituality, ethics, and laws regulating land distribution, ownership, and management. People identify themselves with the place of birth because the connection between spirituality and land applies not only to belief systems, but also to the environment that seeks to maintain harmony between people and the natural world.

A spirituality that does not attach itself to the cosmic experience will be abstract, inconsistent, and ineffective. One could argue that land is spiritually, morally, and culturally shaped, and functions as a center for the life of the community. This explanation provides justification for people who present land claims as a spiritual matter without which a dignified life is impossible. Religious and cultural dimensions justify the claim that the value of land is not limited to market value because it has a potential to accommodate different dimensions of human experience.

Identity, Belonging, and Community

The preceding section focused on the need of interpreting cultural traditions and belief systems with respect to the implications of land management. It presented the meaning of land as a possibility constituted by religious and cultural dimensions. The perspectives of religion and culture portrayed land as a locus of identity, membership, and self-determination. In so doing, land becomes one of the strongest variables that shape the attitude of attachment.[20] This section extends further the argument by linking land rights to the claims of identity, belonging, and community.

The task of defining one's identity is complex because identity is extended to different dimensions of human experience. The existence of relational connections underscores the claim that identity is constituted by traditions, institutions, and communities. In this case land is among the attributes that shape notions of identity, belonging, and community, and for this reason it becomes a dimension that actualizes authenticity. Norms that regulate traditional communities present the claim of ancestral heritage as a testimony that constitutes identity, ownership, and membership. Self-recognition is not limited to ownership; rather, it is extended to the process of becoming a trustee of the cultural heritage. The claim of identity justifies the importance of heritage and continuity. The place of birth forms a part of one's identity, and it cannot be ignored because it forms a part of who a person is. Identity, as a socio-cultural construct, endorses recognition because a collective memory is not limited to the past; rather, it is a part of the present that shapes the future. Such interconnectedness makes identity a resource underlying the claims of belonging and community.

People who share the same identity think of themselves as having a common destiny. Identities are founded upon collective experiences and traditions. They fashion processes of socialization, self-realization, and self-determination, which ultimately constitute value systems, traditions, and worldviews. The unity of a society depends on the shared identity and territory which, in turn, depends on a shared memory. A piece of land that a person owns, as a member of the community, justifies the claim of identity, whether it is an ancestral heritage, place of birth, or a region identified with the myth of origin. When land becomes a determinant variable in all living conditions, disputes over ownership occur. The nature of the collective identities pertains to self-conceptions related to the claims of belonging and community that constitute patterns of social relations. Identities could be exclusive or inclusive depending on the social context.

Traditional communities perceive land as an entitlement entrusted to the community with a condition that it cannot be bought, sold, exchanged, or given to strangers. The following extract, from the report of Eddy Ngeta, makes the argument explicit:

> The Kalenjin and Kikuyu communities are fighting over the land of 585 acres called Rafiki Farm. The Kalenjin claim that the area is part of their ancestral land while the Kikuyu maintain they were allocated the land by the government and will not leave. According to other residents, the Kalenjin have barred other communities from burying their dead in plots they consider their own, even if the land originally belonged to the deceased. This is because, according to the Kalenjin culture, land in which the dead have been interred cannot be transferred.[21]

Identity is not given, nor is it self-evident; rather, it is achieved through the process of socialization, selection, and appropriation. Without appropriation and continuity identity cannot become a foundation of the claims of belonging and community. In order to maintain wholeness and cohesion, a tradition serves as a trustee that guarantees continuity over stretches of time. In such a process land forms a background that sustains the process of socialization. People construct identities as a means of safeguarding collective interests. They do it to strengthen identities that favor their own culture.

The meaning of land bears a wide spectrum pertaining to the values of identity, belonging, and community. Land provides content to the meaning of identity and belonging because it keeps individuals, families, and communities together. Belonging to a particular community has a significant cultural implication. People, especially in rural areas, cannot feel that they belong to a particular community if they do not own a piece of land. A Burundian refugee returning from exile argues that "land connects the current generation to their ancestors. Land, as a gift you have for your descendants, keeps the extended family together, and as such it is like an umbilical cord of the community."[22] Feelings of this sort reinforce the meanings of identity, belonging, and community. It is from such a perspective that land disputes become a part of identity politics.

Assimilation and integration cannot be a sufficient justification for ownership. The place of birth serves as a justification for belonging and operates as a locus around which people form identity. In search for effective methodologies of conflict resolution, for example, people tend to mobilize, identify, and construct myths of origin around their place of birth in order to form a set of shared memories as a way of verifying, strengthening, or justifying the legitimacy of their claims. It is from such perceptions that land becomes a symbol that consolidates identity, belonging, and community.

In traditional communities, a person is worthless without land. The rationale underlying this argument arises from the thinking that land forms a boundary between individuals, groups, and communities. Communities and nations cannot be identified without territories, because identities are tied to specific places that form distinctive references. That is to say land plays a significant role in the process of building personal, familial, communal, and national identities. Inability to own land affects the status of a person, including the ability to produce wealth for one's family. Land ownership generates feelings of self-esteem, status, and autonomy.

Land is not only a territory. It is also an identity constructed by religio-cultural traditions to become a part of the symbolic representation of the world. Human societies have physical and conceptual relations between themselves and environment, because they occupy specific places and tend to justify their occupancy spiritually.[23] These relations are usually expressed by metaphors of homeland, fatherland, motherland, ancestral-land, promised-land, and other similar notions "describing a territory which by nature belongs to a given community expressing feelings and emotions about the essence of land as sacred."[24]

A community commands no respect without land because land has a unique influence on identity and status. It is through the ownership of land that self-respect of a human person is enhanced. Inability to own land requires a person to search for self-worth in other areas of self-realization. The claim of ancestral heritage makes land a distinctive point of reference in terms of authenticity. Land, as a symbolic reference, is conceived as a "common patrimony which reinforces feelings of having identifiable social roots and belonging to a supportive and united human entity."[25] The value of land is presented as a cultural heritage, and individuals return to their place of birth to experience self-identity among other members of the community. One seeks identity in the acquisition of land because it reinforces the claims of belonging, community, and entitlement.

Ownership, Autonomy, and Self-Determination

The preceding discussion established multiple connections that bring together different dimensions of land. At this point it is appropriate to find out how these connections justify the claims of ownership, autonomy, and self-determination.

Land ownership is usually presented under the theme of property rights accompanied with the claim that land is subject to the common purpose, and, as I have argued earlier, private ownership is justified on condition that it is destined for the common good. Large-scale farming that undermines the well-being of a community brings hardship to a people because it disregards the interest of the whole society. Communitarians argue that private property must respect communal well-being by upholding the principle of the common good.[26]

While respecting the right to private ownership we have also to acknowledge that land is created for collective purposes. Despite the importance of the ethical demand for responsible stewardship dualistic tendencies persist. The situation raises a crucial question toward privatization that affects the land issue by concentrating ownership in the hands of a few people. The situation generates anxiety because the way land is distributed does not uphold the principles of stewardship, distributive justice, and the common good. Inclusive traditions of land use designed to challenge eviction, landlessness, exclusion, and greed are no longer operative.

In order to get into the heart of land-related disputes it is appropriate to examine different systems of land ownership. The claim of ownership becomes important when there are competing interests between persons. A person living alone

on an isolated island has no need of laws. The need arises
when another person joins this single individual, that is, when
it becomes necessary to distinguish the property that belongs
to this person from those that belong to the new-comer. The
distinction is necessary in order to determine the boundary of
ownership as well as avoid conflict of interests.

For customary land rights systems, there are two
categories of land ownership, namely, private ownership and
collective ownership. The collective ownership is founded
upon the principles of the collective memory. In this
category, to use the words of Kwame Kuffo, "land belongs to
the community, village, or family, never to the individual.
Neither the individual members of the households nor
community representatives can sell land."[27] Community owns
the land with each individual having a right to use it in a
manner acceptable to the community. There is no permanent
private ownership of land because it belongs to the people as
a whole. The community must own land in order to provide
livelihood to all of its members. This arrangement expresses
the core of the customary land rights systems. In this category
the title of ownership is vested in the corporate body of
which its members reside.

The chief, as local leader, holds land in trust for the
benefit of the community. He has no ultimate authority over
the system of ownership and procedure of distribution of
land to the extent of acting alone.[28] The true owners of the
land are communities. Traditionally, remarks George B.N.
Ayittey,

> The chief was a custodian of the land. His role was to
> hold the land in trust. He could not deny tribesmen
> access to the land. Even strangers could obtain use rights
> upon the provision of a token gift. User rights were

accorded so long as a small tribute was paid and the land was not abused. If a family abandoned their farmland and moved out of the tribal areas, as was often the case, such unoccupied land fell into the custody of the chief for reallocation. The chief would not claim ownership of this land even though the people might refer to it as belonging to the chief.[29]

Traditional communities regarded themselves as being held together by ancestral land. Collective ownership stifles private ownership as a means of discouraging accumulation, selfishness, and greed. Since the customary land rights are founded upon communitarian value systems, the power of the land ownership was vested within the community with the power to administer the rights of ownership and use.

The meaning of land as a community asset derives from the claim that it is a cultural heritage that must be preserved and transferred from one generation to another by inheritance. It is an asset to which an individual cannot be permitted to lay an absolute claim on it. Collective ownership is the only category that can be considered to be complete.

In order to comprehend the relationship between ownership and autonomy it is appropriate to examine the scope of the customary land rights. Land is a determinant variable in the process of constructing cultural identities and organizing belief systems. The link between generations is determined by the land shared by families and communities. It is not possible to advocate claims of identity, community, autonomy, and self-determination without territory.[30]

In many cultures, the right to inheritance is not accorded to women. This tradition draws its justification from the conviction that women are dependent, and for security purposes they must be grouped together with children. In

14

spelling out the subordination of women to men within the family, Benjamin Kiriswa writes:

The father is not only perceived as the protector and head of the family; he is also the sole authority whose commands and expectations have to be followed by every member of the family. In most African homes dialogue is almost non-existent. The father is vested with all the authority for decision-making. There is no power sharing in the family. The father does not show his love either to the wife or children, making them fearful and uneasy with him. The father is always portrayed as a brutal figure in the family. The mother is exactly the opposite: passive and submissive. She is expected to listen and implement whatever she is told to do without any question in spite of bearing most of the burden in the family. In some communities mothers are regarded as children; and they can be battered, tortured, or send away at will by their husbands. Mothers are not seen as companions; on the contrary, they are regarded as chattels, property, and means to an end.[31]

On the husband's death women are left without anything for support even though they may have young children to care for, and as a result some of them "become destitute unless they have children to whom they can turn to for support."[32] The following extract from Aili Tripp, drawn from the Ugandan customary land rights literature, makes the argument incisive:

Customary rules have the tendency of excluding females from the clan or community entity, which excludes females from ownership. Attempts by women to control property, especially land, are considered by the community as misbehavior. A woman who buys land is seen as having sinister intentions either to run away from her marital home, or use it as a place to entertain other men. The threat of women gaining power through property ownership makes society frown upon women who go ahead to acquire property of their own. Proper women are satisfied with males being the provider in their lives, and they take whatever is provided to them with gratitude, and teach their daughters to do the same.[33]

These observations confirm the argument that customary land rights do not accord women due respect as persons who can own property.

The rationale of denying the right of ownership to women is based upon three arguments. First, land must be inherited through a male who owns it on behalf of the family. Second, ancestral land cannot be transferred to another family, clan, or community through marriage. Third, women are considered to be temporary members of the family because of the possibility of divorce. As a way of denying the negative consequences that may arise from this custom, proponents of the customary land rights claim that it is not true that rights of women are violated. Widows and divorced women are taken care of by the extended family.

Whatever justifications put forward in defense of the traditional systems of inheritance, it does not seem appropriate in the modern world to apply customary land rights without reform.[34] To do so would be the same as perpetuating the tradition of gender inequality. Customary land rights systems face a strong opposition arising from the changing conditions of life. In many ways they have failed to reform themselves so as to remain relevant. The international standards of human rights regard property ownership for women as a right, whether they are married or not.

If the rights of women are to be realized, then customary rights must be reformed. The dynamics of the customary land rights should go beyond the traditional framework that entails gender discrimination. In advocating structural change, the United Nations Habitat claims that implementation of human rights ideals is difficult due to the lack of institutional reform and cultural change.[35] Change is often perceived as a threat to cultural traditions.

In order to defend the rights of women we have to establish a framework that can provide protection for the victims of gender discrimination. To support the argument, Nyokabi Kamau writes:

> Modern social organization should have laws that are women-friendly and that recognize their unique circumstances as a result of their gender. All people, not just women's organizations, must get involved in creating awareness of the problem. The violated persons should be made aware that they need not feel ashamed of the problem. Men and women need to be given training on these issues so that one understands the problem from the wider perspective.[36]

We must all be involved in challenging traditions that continue to practice gender discrimination.

Land disputes emerge when there are different value systems with different definitions of land. In English culture, for example, different interests can exist over the same piece of land; meaning that different people can hold different interests on the same piece of land. Organization of this kind is foreign to Africa. Comparatively, the English system of

17

land ownership "emphasizes private ownership of land while the African customary system of law emphasizes communal ownership of land. Because of the difference in emphasis, there is bound to be a conflict."[37] Differences derive from the fact that land ownership is defined with reference to detachment of the individual from the community and pursuit of the market value. Using this template for African customary land ownership systems "is unsatisfactory, because access to land is linked to the sovereign community."[38] The right of ownership under customary land rights systems serves multiple meanings and functions as opposed to the market approach. The difference in perception is compounded with the conflict of meanings between different land rights systems, which renders the effort of formulating integral land law elusive.

Because of the diversity of value systems, customary land rights differ from one community to another. People depend on the collective memory of the community to resolve disputes. In case of a dispute, remarks Smoking Wanjala, the collective memory is established through "elderly witnesses who are presumed to know what must have taken place."[39] Land disputes remain unresolved when the registration system overshadows customary land rights. To conclude the argument, Wanjala makes a compelling remark:

> Many people in the rural areas are influenced by customary notions of landholding. At the time of adjudication, consolidation, and registration, people did not and still do not understand the full impact of individualization of tenure. It is because of this that we have many disputes between registered owners and other claimants. As long as customary land laws hold firm in the minds of the people alongside the government's

vigorous policy to individualize tenure through registration, there will be many disputes over land ownership.[40]

The system of registration becomes problematic when statutory land law confines justice to the owner who has a title deed.

The conflict between customary and statutory land rights systems is evident in five ways: first, the high court and the court of appeal operate as different systems of law; second, it is not clear how the courts decide when disputes include a registered private owner, a family trustee, and unregistered claimant; third, land transfer systems are unclear because they involve three competing legal systems, namely, customary, private, and statutory; fourth, land disputes occur as a result of provisions of law, some of which are unclear and do not coincide with the aspirations of the African traditions; and fifth, where farmland is scarce, the state control is seen as an infringement on right of autonomy of traditional communities.

The transfer of court cases from one court to another shows that there is a conflict between different law systems that regulate land ownership. In the course of interpreting this practice, ordinary people think that the process occurs in order to engage competent lawyers handling the cases. But the truth of the matter is that moving from one court system to another involves moving from one system of law to another. The problem could be resolved by answering these questions: which system of land rights, between customary and statutory, should be preserved? Is it possible to form an integrated system of land ownership derived from the two systems?

19

To change the situation, argues Arthur Okoth Owino, there must be an overall review of the land rights systems with a view to overhaul all procedures pertaining to land administration so as to establish an economically-efficient, socially-equitable, and environmentally-friendly land use system that is free from manipulation.[41] The lack of secure land rights systems "holds back economic development, perpetuates poverty, and fans social tensions. Economic progress cannot be achieved until the issue of land rights is addressed."[42]

Sentiments of self-preservation, in certain contexts and circumstances, create a condition in which certain communities are perceived as foreigners who deserve eviction. It is an attitude motivated by the politics of competition that uses ethnic identity as a territorial boundary. Sometimes identity differences are used as a means to advocate eviction of the minority communities from the areas considered to exclusively belong to certain communities. Competition for land advocates identity politics that requires those considered to be outsiders to return to their "ancestral province and if for any reason they would be reluctant to do so, they would by all means be forced to do so."[43]

The increase of land disputes is aggravated by ineffective judiciary systems. As Ahmednasir Abdulahi has put it, "judiciary is the third important arm of the government. But it has not played its lawful role in the past."[44] Judiciary has become a discredited institution whose role has been eroded by political manipulation, inefficiency, and corruption. It is not an exaggeration to say that justice has become a commodity for sale. With the increasing practice of corruption in public institutions, courts have been converted into judicial bazaars, thereby making people lose their confidence in the judiciary. Courts, at all levels, are also used by the ruling class as a means of maintaining status quo, inequality, and impunity. Corruption is common among judges who are widely regarded as guardians of the law.[45] Judicial systems, under these conditions, are destroyed by political manipulation and institutional interference. Without a structural overhaul of the existing judiciary systems it is unrealistic to count on the role of the judiciary in the reform of land rights systems.

Courts are reluctant to go beyond the outdated legal systems we inherited from the colonial administration, even in the light of evidence of false documentation and corruption in the allocation process. Evidence of a title deed, whether dubiously obtained or not, defeats a move geared to challenge illegal transactions. A number of judges, coupled with the problem of corruption, use the weaknesses of the judiciary system for enrichment. They are more preoccupied with small-scale disputes for private interest than addressing the root causes of the problem. The need to serve justice is simply not their primary concern. The law-breakers are in favor of the situation because it enables them to delay any attempt geared toward changing unjust policies. Although the abuse of public land has been made known there has been limited political will to prosecute those involved because the people involved are politically-connected.

In recent years, as witnessed in many countries, land disputes have intensified because existing land laws cannot handle modern problems. Law enforcement, which is intended to protect the rights of the citizen, does not function efficiently because of institutional corruption and political interference. The judiciary turns a blind eye to the forced evictions of the indigenous people from their ancestral land. Due to widespread negligence, incompetence, and corruption in the courts, most cases are never heard through completion. Where lawlessness is rampant self-interest overshadows the rule of law.

Land is a "concept that expresses itself in social relations."[46] The claims of ownership and autonomy cannot be properly understood without making reference to the customary land rights. The claims of land ownership are complex because they emerge from different value systems. Ownership refers to the rights-claims over a piece of land.

For Akan people, observes Kuffo, "selling land is synonymous to the act of selling a spiritual heritage, which is a betrayal of ancestral trust and an undoing of the hope of prosperity."[47] Foreign systems of access and ownership of the land make land a commodity for sale.[48] The strategy of selling land rights to foreign investors and confining citizens to slums represent contemporary Africa at its worst. These trends are connected to the individualization and privatization of land rights. This process is facilitated by the requirement of title registration to procure security. Foreign land ownership systems introduced ethical and legal confusion in the way of defining land.

Customary land rights systems are respected at the grassroots level for various reasons. They are considered to be flexible and efficient in resolving disputes at the grassroots level as well as providing assured security in contrast to the statutory land rights which are considered to be alien, inefficient, and inaccessible. Customary justice systems, comparatively, have played a role of maintaining healthy social relations because they are quick in resolving disputes, while the statutory land rights systems are inaccessible and unfamiliar to many people. Despite the need of unified land law compromise has not been forthcoming.

Customary and statutory land rights, from an ideological comparison, maintain a longstanding contradiction.

Customary land rights systems presented as models that are contextual-bound, authentically-rooted in religio-cultural traditions, and economically-identified with peasantry. But critics argue that customary land rights systems "hold the match toward civilization backward" because of their attachment to obsolete cultural traditions, whereas the statutory land rights systems are presented as a model that transcends time, context, and cultural differences. They present themselves as progressive models that can address modern challenges of land management as well as advance ways that can liberate people from poverty.

The relevancy of customary land rights, despite this appraisal, remains comparatively weak, and recently it has come under severe criticism. The significance of the customary land rights systems have, therefore, come under severe scrutiny recently. Criticisms have emerged because of the existing confusion between informal and formal systems of land ownership. Critics argue that customary land rights systems are inconsistent, unpredictable, and discriminatory.

From the standpoint of Marcel Rutter, "traditional African land tenure systems induce inefficient allocation of resources because property rights are not clearly defined."[49] These criticisms have emerged because of the inability to accommodate large-scale farming. Land ownership is limited to the blood relations, whereby the land is vested in a descent group, and access is determined by ethnic identity with the possibility of consolidating exclusive rights of ownership. Others argue that customary land rights emerge from insecure ownership that renders farmers incapable of developing the land they occupy with a long-term strategy.

The emergence of distinct communities is a consequence of the emergence of exaggerated importance of cultural differences. The search for autonomy and self-determination compel every social group, irrespective of size, to preserve its identity. A desire of this magnitude arises from the fact that every community has a way of working to consolidate cultural uniformity to guarantee its survival. Identity and territory have become foundational components required for consolidating autonomy. They generate a distinction between natives and migrants with numerically stronger communities attempting to reassert their dominance.

From the viewpoint of social relations, disputes over land arise when there is a history of injustice. Identity is used as a means of social, political, and religious mobilization. Its claims are extended to the political sphere where intensification of the attitude of self-identification and exclusion become important. Different communities have different value systems that entail claims of autonomy and self-determination. Disordered relations between communities arise from the struggle for autonomy and self-determination. The inter-communal conflicts in a number of countries, such as Tanzania, Kenya, and Burundi, have been increasing and prevail in different forms. The claims of territorial integrity and self-determination are contextual and complex variables attached to the claims of autonomy and self-determination.

We can sum up the weaknesses of the customary land rights into seven categories: first, the scope of the customary land rights exclude women and migrants from the right of ownership; second, land ownership is limited to blood relations; third, ownership system based on blood relations is problematic because it is not inclusive; fourth, the lack of formal documentation does not attract long-term investment; fifth, customary land rights do not pay attention about the limits of its scope, policy development, and relevancy in the modern world; sixth, allocation policies are not clearly defined; and seventh, peasants and herders are not constrained by the responsibility of environmental conservation.[50] These observations show that the reform of customary land rights is required.

Looking at the claim of self-determination one could argue that the right to self-determination propagates a desire to be distinctive, and presents entitlement and autonomy as a means of self-assertion. Traditionally, the legitimacy of membership is based on the claim of common identity confined within a given territory. The criterion of territory demarcation is essential for the process of building a personal image of oneself expressed in terms of identity, self-esteem, and autonomy. Identity entitles people to the rights of belonging, ownership, and membership. These claims are interwoven together. The reason is that the claims of identity and belonging are founded upon collective experiences that entail interdependency. The connection between generations is identified using the claim of belonging to specific families, clans, and communities. These claims contribute to the ongoing process of reshaping the politics of belonging, ownership, and wealth distribution. It is inconceivable to think of strengthening identity, autonomy, and self-determination of the community without a territory.

The right to self-determination is one of the most complex entitlements in asserting the claim of autonomy. The situation arises from the argument that communities invoke the right to self-determination as a means of asserting themselves. The right to self-determination accords communities the right to control their own destiny. Although self-determination is evoked from the viewpoint of human rights, it is not clear how such a claim could be concretized. The point of contention is that the meaning of self-determination does not automatically entail autonomy, secession, or statehood. The rights of belonging, autonomy, and self-determination are essential for human flourishing. The self is constructed in relation to selves, and the memory founded upon identities can be justified insofar as it promotes the common good.

The right to self-determination is founded upon the principle of freedom that upholds that all human beings are entitled to exist as autonomous persons. The need of autonomy justifies the claim of self-esteem as a necessary condition for human flourishing. This claim refers to freedom as a foundation for self-realization and self-determination. The need of autonomy underscores the right to organize one's own life. The desire for it presupposes authority of each person in the process of making decisions. Self-determination, as a motivation toward selfhood, depends upon the fact that human beings participate in social life by being able to choose the kind of actions to undertake, values to pursue, and means to use. It is a kind of engagement that requires a well-thought-out plan chosen by a free moral agent.

Autonomy refers to the ability of making decisions about one's life. It is the foundation of the claims of self-esteem, self-realization, and self-determination. This requirement mandates the argument that all individuals, regardless of cultural context, must have access to those conditions under which they are able to live as autonomous moral agents capable of selecting and pursuing objectives that are in accordance with one's conception of the good.

The claim of autonomy is important when minority groups are deprived of their rights of participation, autonomy, and self-determination. It is important to note that any political organization that overlooks the autonomy of the local communities to govern their own life would be categorized as an unjust system. It is from such a perspective that we can say land-grabbing is a way of impoverishing people because it removes them from their livelihood.

Is it possible to define the meaning of self-determination with a focus on people instead of territory so as to avoid the possibility of linking self-determination to secession? African countries gained international sovereignty by virtue of decolonization. The claim of secession could be linked to different reasons. The secession of Somaliland amid continued clan-based fighting provides a good example for secession politics. When the state is weakened its ability to resist secession movements is reduced. Exclusion and inequality in the public sphere affect relations between communities with a possibility of intensifying the feelings of discontentment. These conditions are often linked to secession claims, as diversity generates cleavages that could lead to political fragmentation. Discrimination increases the level of polarization and competition for political and economic control.

Privatization of Land Rights

Can land rights be privatized? To answer the question, it is appropriate to begin by saying that land is different from other goods. Private ownership is perceived as a monopoly on the use of the community land. Land becomes a private property when individuals declare it private and choose to enforce monopoly in the way of owning and using it. Is there any reasonable justification for this claim? John Locke puts forth the idea of improvement as a justification for private ownership.[51] He argues that improving a piece of public land gives the person who improves it the right of ownership. In this case, the argument of improvement justifies private ownership.[52]

In Africa, community owns land with its members having a right to use it in a manner acceptable to all. There is no permanent private ownership of land because land, as a collective heritage, belongs to the community as a whole. There are three justifications worth of note here: first, the community owns land to provide a means of living for all of its members; second, land is entrusted to the community for the future generations; and third, land cannot be owned privately on permanent basis for the purpose of accumulation and self-interest. These arguments justify the claim that commoditization, commercialization, and privatization of land are foreign to the African cultures.

In challenging private ownership, Julius Nyerere, the first President of the Republic of Tanzania, argued:

> To us in Africa land was always recognized as belonging to the community. Each individual within our society had a right to the use of land, because otherwise he could not earn his living, and one cannot have the right to life without also having the right to some means of maintaining life. But the African's right to land was simply the right to use it; he had no other right to it, nor did it occur to him to try and claim one. The foreigner introduced a completely different concept, the concept of land as a marketable commodity. According to this system, a person could claim a piece of land as his own private property whether he intended to use it or not. I could take a few square miles of land, call them "mine"; and then go off to the moon. All I had to do to gain a living from "my" land was to charge a rent to the people who wanted to use it. If this piece of land was in an urban area I had no need to develop it all; I could leave it to the fools who were prepared to develop all the other pieces

28

of land surrounding "my" piece, and in doing so, automatically raise the market value of mine. Then I could come down from the moon and demand these fools pay me through their noses for the high value of "my" land, a value that they themselves had created for me while I was enjoying myself on the moon. Such a system is not only foreign to us, it is completely wrong. Landlords, in a society that recognizes individual ownership of land, can be, and usually are, in the same class as the loiterers I was talking about, the class of parasites.[53]

The argument of Nyerere unfolds the growing tension between private ownership and communal ownership. Although there are numerous critiques on land ownership systems that forewarn of the emergence of the tragedy of commoditization, commercialization and privatization, African countries have been slow to acknowledge that allowing private land ownership system, without proper regulations, could be problematic.

The Universal Declaration of Human Rights states that "everyone has the right to own property alone as well as in association with others. No one shall be arbitrarily deprived of his property."[54] This guideline confirms the connection that exists between private ownership and collective ownership. Proponents of privatization argue that private ownership is a reliable guarantee for freedom and self-realization. Without assurance of private ownership, writes Olivier De Schutter, large-scale farmers and small-scale farmers, alike, cannot attain the courage required to develop permanent structures on the land they occupy.[55] Private ownership is useful because it encourages individuals to be creative, productive, and responsible. Those who oppose privatization, on the other hand, argue that private ownership, when it is unchallenged, undermines collective rights.

Small-scale farmers, for African countries, occupy a prominent role in feeding the population.[56] To allow multinational corporations to displace them would aggravate poverty because most of the produce from the large-scale farming is destined to the food market of the wealthy countries. In collaboration with agribusiness corporations private ownership allows landholding in terms of private estates and transfer of capital and profit from one country to another. Multinational corporations are more focused on maximizing profit than the welfare of the citizens and environmental conditions.

Forces of privatization threaten the well-being of the vulnerable people. In East Africa, for example, vast areas of common grazing lands, once accessible to the Maasai people, are now fenced off.[57] Large portions of land have been privatized, sold, or leased for touristic ventures, "giving rise to fears that this is just the beginning of a new form of colonization."[58] Some of them are now grazing their cattle on the semi-arid areas. Under these circumstances it remains unclear how they would survive in the future. The emerging trend of land-grabbing for large-scale farming is progressively displacing small-scale farmers and herders from their land with a possibility of rendering them landless, unemployed, or casual laborers.[59]

Kaj Ahren, from the standpoint of the pastoral peoples, argues that "the relationship between the colonial state and the indigenous peoples has been replaced by the structurally similar relationship of internal colonialism between the post-colonial state and the pastoral peasantry."[60] Conditions of forced migration, eviction, and landlessness are gradually intensifying. These challenges remind us that discriminatory land rights systems currently in place must be changed. These changes must empower legal systems to protect vulnerable people from the market forces.[61]

Land disputes are increasing because foreign investors are taking land for speculation. In a context where land is becoming scarce, seemingly,

> The creation of a market for land rights encourages speculation, and the small-scale farmers could easily be priced out. Small-scale farmers could be forced to resort to distress sales, particularly if they have fallen in debt as a result of an occasional bad harvest.[62]

The practice of land titling without capital to develop it, remarks De Shutter, increases the vulnerability of the small-scale farmers by allowing "foreign investors to pressure smallholders into selling the most productive and mineral rich land."[63] A number of studies have shown that land reform favors well-financed entrepreneurs coming from abroad.[64] That is to say there is a tendency to ignore small-scale formers in favor of commercial farmers with a long-term investment.

The rate of leasing land to foreign investors without consent of the indigenous people could be a source of conflict. The argument of Obang Metho, below, is prudent about the outcome:

> No one should believe that foreign investors are there to feed starving Africans, create jobs, or improve food security. Selling land rights cannot guarantee progress for local people and will not lead to food in their stomachs.

These deals lead only to dollars in the pockets of corrupt leaders and foreign investors.[65]

A genuine investment requires accountability. It is, however, unfair to blame foreigners for the problems considered to emerge from the local situation. Oppression is not possible without collaboration of the oppressed. The priority of the poor countries should be to feed themselves rather than having to buy food from abroad or rely on food aid to feed their people.[66] Selling land rights to foreign investors cannot automatically overcome poverty. What we need, as a long-term solution, are investments that do not destroy peasantry. Investments that generate employment do not necessarily cause displacement, eviction, or landlessness.

It is not right to grant public land to investors without the consent of the people concerned. A practice of this sort endangers the lives of the small-scale farmers. Large-scale investment should not destroy the livelihood of the small-farmers. Rather, it must be organized in such a way that it benefits everyone by involving the local population. Grabbing public land becomes possible when public officials facilitate secrecy around the procedure of registration and transfer.[67] Clearly, there is something that has gone awfully wrong within the ranks of public administration.

Statutory land rights systems bear several weaknesses. It is interesting to note that statutory land rights systems are more interested with foreign investors than citizens. It is unjust to remove indigenous people from their land in order to accommodate foreign investors.[68] In the case of Loliondo, Tanzania, for example, the government has been trying to evict the Maasai people from their ancestral land to create a ground for hunting sport.[69] Unfettered privatization of land rights cannot be profitable because the poor cannot be a part of the market forces.

The idea of introducing foreign investment to increase agricultural production is not an ill-founded idea. The problem arises from the weak administration at the level of public institutions. Those in positions of authority use the situation by using the power entrusted to them to facilitate eviction and land-grabbing, thereby relegating the local population to the rank of casual laborers. The trends of land-grabbing and eviction of the indigenous people from their land would result into the formation of a class of people who are landless and unemployed.

Unfettered privatization encourages land-grabbers and speculators to hold the state hostage by planting their own agents in the public institutions to facilitate decisions which favor their own agenda. The process generates a condition whereby the needy are deprived of their livelihood. Privatization of land rights works in favor of those who know how to manipulate the law. The ruling class has access to the legal systems and connections to the policymakers and financial institutions. Small-scale farmers, on the contrary, are defenseless when their land is taken by investors under the assistance of the government.

In several cases, due to the lack of public accountability on the part of the government, small-scale farmers may not know what is happening until it is too late. With limited understanding of formal legal procedure and lack of financial support, small-scale farmers have no chance to defend their right of ownership. It is increasingly becoming clear that land is not allocated to genuine developers, but to speculators, agribusiness corporations, and politically-connected individuals.

The traditional way of life, with limited ability to understand the formal legal procedure, cannot challenge the wave of land-grabbing generated by agribusiness corporations. The loss of livelihood goes together with the increasing migration to the slums of the metropolitan cities. The influx of the displaced people joins the ranks of the landless and unemployed people. The state bears responsibility for granting land to investors without considering the condition of the citizens. The resulting consequences generate disputes that may last for a long time. In search for a long-term solution to the problem, the next section examines the initiatives of land reform.

Initiatives of Land Reform

Formalization of land rights and investment are considered to be necessary in order to increase productivity. Economists believe that land reform can transform peasantry into a reliable sector for employment and wealth creation. They see the emergence of the financial market as having a beneficial impact on the use of land to increase production.

Land reform intends to improve conditions that obstruct access and ownership of land for disadvantaged people. It focuses on reallocation, security tenure, productivity, and management as a means of improving the life of the poor. Conditions that necessitate land reform include population growth, land-grabbing, ethnic-cleansing, and environmental degradation. Meanwhile, there have been limited initiatives devoted to land reform since independence. The situation has been caused by the lack of political will, inability to investigate the nature of the existing land-related disputes, and the lack of locally-formulated methodologies that can facilitate social action. The commonly used methodologies of land reform have not been operative in many parts of Africa.

According to Ambreena Manji, "land reform has not taken place in a uniformly linear fashion. Instead, the pace of change has been uneven, the process often fractured and incoherent."[70] Where it has taken place the absence of landless, peasant organizations, consultative procedures in the process of making new land laws, and selling land rights to foreign investors have tarnished initiatives of land reform. Elsewhere, implementation of new land laws has been lacking, slow, or ineffective. From the commercial viewpoint, another weakness arises from the condition that

> Bankers' organizations have had a central place in determining the shape and content of Africa's new land laws. The liberalization of land markets and the promotion of formal credit provide unprecedented opportunities for commercial lenders. They have tried to ensure that new land laws do not increase the risks entailed in lending. Reports emanating from some African countries suggest that the concerns of commercial lenders have been taken up by politicians.[71]

Land reform has been viewed as a part of the decolonization process and important step toward socio-economic development. Yet, for more than six decades, there are few methodologies that could be applied to motivate initiatives of land redistribution. From an administrative standpoint, most of the existing land reform initiatives concentrate on data collection to produce reports that become the end of the project. The lack of courage to implement recommendations has left the question of land disputes largely unresolved.[72] The need of land reform began before independence, under which land in the hands of a few people was addressed, but, to the present day, the problem has not been resolved.[73]

There is no doubt that land reform is a prerequisite for economic development and peaceful social relations. But many countries are unwilling to address the problem. Land reform has not been taken seriously except as a political propaganda designed to solicit votes during the periods of general elections. The idea of creating a separate customary legal system that operates side-by-side with statutory land rights has become a source of confusion. The pressure comes from "the demands of the international market which has created incoherent and outward-looking economic structures of dependency."[74]

Land reform involves changing regulations of distribution, ownership, and use. It is a project that entails evaluation of the benefits, consequences, and participation of the people concerned. Without a clear procedure it could be a source of conflict. The process must be undertaken carefully because it is a political process that affects regulations of resource distribution and social relations. The meaning of land could be a source of conflict due to the differences that exist between cultural traditions and life conditions. Similarly, electoral mobilization and the use of land as a patronage resource to motivate land reform efforts, as it has been witnessed in the extensive land reforms in Zimbabwe, cannot be a long-term solution.[75] People of Zimbabwe, it could be said, resorted to dramatic land reforms to fulfill the purpose of fighting for independence.[76] But, as Bill Derman and Anne Hellum conclude, "the Zimbabwe's effort at land reform remains highly contested."[77]

Land reform cannot be carried out in isolation from the struggles of democratization because unjust methodologies of land distribution "produce social, economic, and political inequalities."[78] Access to land depends on the influence one has over the systems of land rights.[79] It means that conditions that determine access to land depend on different conditions of life. It is not possible to resolve land disputes without knowing the root causes within a given context. African land rights are "intimately wrapped up with kinship relations."[80] Land reform is a process of redefining social relations.

Studies undertaken recently in Southern Sudan suggest that in order to avoid conflict over land distribution, ownership, and management we must acknowledge that

> Land belongs to the community, and that community land cannot be sold. The historical injustices that have been condoned in the name of investment and national economic growth should never be allowed to take deep roots in the South Sudan. It is better to live poor and closer to nature in a community owned land than let go the community land in the name of modern advancement in infrastructure that is only affordable and disposable to the rich.[81]

If the community land is transferred to state ownership there is a risk of being managed by irresponsible leaders as it has happened in many countries. The state governance is corrupt, but a community cannot draw itself into such conduct. As a way of guaranteeing community benefits, following the framework of the common good, the way of proceeding must ensure that land ownership remains with the local people who can manage it more responsibly than public institutions.[82]

Claims of land ownership become controversial when the way of defining distribution, ownership, and management vary from one culture to another. It suffices to note that land is a political process because it confers political power in the process of allocation. Some arguments in support of land reform focus on the need to get rid of conflicting land rights where statutory and customary land rights systems exist in tension with each other. Meanwhile the confusion over which set of land rights systems has primacy over others remains unsettled. It is evident that conflicting land rights weakens legal systems by making them prone to manipulation. The project of land reform cannot be carried out without some difficulties because it could be advantageous to certain communities while at the same time victimizing others.[83] The difficulty accompanying reform initiatives arises from the possibility of transferring land from one community to another.

Customary and statutory land rights systems remain problematic because both are prone to mismanagement.[84] If this is the case then, can customary land rights merge with statutory land rights? Is it possible to form an integral land law that can avoid the existing legal weaknesses? Appropriate answers to these questions would be valuable. Land reform is limited since there are no clear methodologies spelling out how reform programs can accommodate diverse claims of ownership. True reform must be accompanied with a change of administrative procedure in order to overcome bureaucracy, inefficiency, and corruption.

In many countries, where land disputes are experienced, there are people endowed with passion to work for change, "but usually they are defeated by the powerful internal forces stacked against them."[85] The ruling class use their political influence and financial clout to oppose change. "Although the reformers have truth on their side, truth is just another special interest. The villains are willing to lie in order to defeat change and have an advantage over those constrained by honesty."[86] Whatever the case genuine reforms come from within. Initiatives of reform require rationally-informed methodologies that can shape cultural traditions and public institutions. These methodologies must give reasons for reform, and limitations must be clearly spelled out in advance. A land commission could be setup to look into contentious issues, including the claims of displacement and eviction. Land commissions must be able to produce the outcome in time as well as outline methodologies of resolving the problem. This is important because national commissions are sometimes formed as a strategy designed to delay justice.

The need of comprehensive land rights must be sought as a means of understanding the relationship between cultural identity, good governance, and economic development. The need to undertake reforms cannot be ignored because of the widespread complaints surrounding land distribution, use, and management. It could be beneficial if reforms focus on eliminating unemployment and proper use of land. This project entails the need of addressing the conflict between land rights systems. Conflicting statutory and customary land rights make the existing legal systems on matters pertaining to land management unclear and vulnerable to corruption. Socio-economic and political struggles between different communities could victimize certain individuals, communities, or transfer land from one community to another to satisfy ideological, cultural, or religious loyalty. The lack of institutional capacity to undertake the project is caused by patrimonial politics and institutional corruption that overshadow possibilities of commitment and efficiency. Other areas of concern include environmental degradation, landholding for speculation, and inability to use land productively.

Some of the existing initiatives of land reform are foreign, artificial, and ineffective because they do not emerge from a local context, and methodologies applied are unfamiliar and irrelevant to local needs, contexts, and cultures.[87] For instance, the method of asking concerned governments to buy land from landholding individuals, and then distribute it to the landless is unrealistic. Kenya, Zimbabwe, and Namibia failed to apply this method due to a lack of funds and politically-related disagreements that cropped-up intensified the problem. The truth is that one cannot exactly scratch the itch on the back of another. The person offering the service might end-up scratching the part which is not itching, and consequently the person receiving the service might experience pain instead of relief. Land reform does not mean moving from collective ownership to private ownership, from customary land rights to statutory land rights, or from savage systems to civilized systems. Rather, it is about creating balanced systems of land distribution, ownership, use, and management in view of motivating wealth creation.

Land disputes are always connected to value systems, political organization, and economic conditions. This network shows that access to land is a constitutive component of social relations. The challenge amounts to the process of restructuring social organization.[88] The situation arises when land management is "seen in the context of a wholesale restructuring of the social formation."[89] Land disputes are complex because they are integrated within the patterns of social relations, political organization, cultural traditions, and belief systems. Land disputes are not limited to one dimension of social life; rather, they are situated within the trends of ownership systems, population growth, changing settlement patterns, and class formation.[90] These conditions remind us that land disputes cannot be confined to a single question, ideology, or institution. For a meaningful reform to take place there must be a concerted effort intended to re-conceptualize the meaning, value, and function of land.

The questions raised is an invitation to think critically about state responsibility toward the management of the public land. Also, there is a need to examine the root causes that led to the resistance of the post-colonial leadership to reform the systems we inherited from the past. It is not by looking in the other direction that the challenge would be resolved. When it comes to pressing issues "silence is an unacceptable offense."[91] The state must seek to address historical injustices, heal the wounds of the past, and build institutions based upon the ideals of social justice and human rights. The legitimacy of state is based upon the will of the people, and as such every citizen must be protected, and effort must be made to improve conditions of life for the benefit of all.

Notes

[1] Mach Dzislaw, *Symbol, Conflict, and Identity: Essays in Political Anthropology* (New York: State University of New York Press, 1993), 174.

[2] Ibid., 178.

[3] John Hart, *The Spirit of Earth: A Theology of Land* (New York: Paulist Press, 1984), 111.

[4] Biblical references alluded here are found in the books of Leviticus 25:28 and Deuteronomy 25:19-22.

[5] Frank Brennan, S.J., "Land Rights," in Judith A. Dwyer, ed., *The New Dictionary of Catholic Social Thought* (Minnesota: The Liturgical Press, 1994), 544.

[6] The Book of Leviticus, 25:23.

[7] See, for example, the works of John S. Mbiti, *African Religions and Philosophy* (London: Heinemann Educational Publication, 1990); J.B. Danquah, *The Akan Doctrine of God* (New York: Humanities Press, Inc., 1968).

[8] A clear account on the sacredness of land, from the African perspective, is given by John S. Mbiti, "African Views of the Universe," in Roger S. Gottlies, ed., *The Sacred Earth: Religion, Nature, Environment* (New York: Routledge, 1996), 174-180.

[9] Jomo Kenyatta, *Facing Mount Kenya* (London: Vintage Books, 1938), 22.

[10] Ibid., 27.

[11] Patrick E. Nmah, "Spiritual Dimension of Land Identity Crisis in Igboland of Nigeria," *Unizik Journal of Arts and Humanities* 12, 2 (January 2011): 136-151, at 136.

[12] The introduction of foreign land ownership systems, forcefully, disrupted the traditional customs by ignoring the spiritual connection that exists between people and land.

[13] Nmah, "Spiritual Dimension of Land Identity Crisis in Igboland of Nigeria," 136.

[14] Ibid., 137-138.

[15] Ward Anseeuw and Chris Alden, "Introduction," in Ward Anseeuw and Chris Alden, eds., *The Struggle Over Land in Africa: Conflicts, Politics, and Change* (Cape Town: Human Sciences Research Council, 2010), 1-15, at 2.

[16] Justice A.M. Akiwumi, "Report of the Judicial Commission Appointed to Inquire into Tribal Clashes in Kenya: Rift Valley," *Daily Nation, Kenya* (October 19, 2002): 12-26, at 13.

[17] Nmah, "Spiritual Dimension of Land Identity Crisis in Igboland of Nigeria," 141.

[18] Garric Small and John Sheehan, "Selling Your Family: Why Customary Title is Incomparable to Western Conceptions of Property Value," *http://www.academia.edu/1396111/selling_Your_Family_Why_customary_title_is_incomparable_to_Western_Conceptions_of_Propety_value* (Accessed October 20, 2013).

[19] See, for example, the myth of the Yoruba people of Nigeria which uphold that human beings were created out of clay. This myth is found in a dictionary dedicated to creation myths authored by David A. Leeming and Margaret A. Leeming, *A Dictionary of Creation Myths* (Oxford: Oxford University Press, 2001).

[20] A thesis on land as a central variable to the ideology of attachment is presented by Parker Shipton, *Mortgaging the Ancestors: Ideologies of Attachment in Africa* (New Haven: Yale University Press, 2009), 20, 59-73, 109-129.

[21] Eddy Ngeta, "Leaders Fear Land Feuds in Rift Valley Could Fuel Poll Violence," *Daily Nation, Kenya* (October 19, 2012): 32.

[22] Lucy Hovil, "Citizenship and Land: A Potent Relationship," *http://www.africanaarguments.org/2009/12/14/citizenship-and-land-a-potent-relationship* (Accessed December 21, 2013).

[23] Dzislaw, *Symbol, Conflict, and Identity: Essays in Political Anthropology*, 173.

43

[24] Ibid.

[25] Norman Long, *Family and Work in Rural Societies: Perspectives on Non-Wage Labour* (London: Tavistock Publications, 1984), 20.

[26] Pope John Paul II, *Solicitudo Rei Socialis*, 42.

[27] Olivier De Schutter, "How Not to Think of Land-Grabbing: Three Critiques of Large-Scale Investments in Farmland," *Journal of Peasant Studies* 38, 2 (March 2011): 249-279, at 271.

[28] Kwame Akuffo, "The Conception of Land Ownership in African Customary Law and Its Implication for Development," *African Journal of International and Comparative Law* 17, 1 (March 2009): 57-78, at 271

[29] George B.N. Ayittey, *Indigenous African Institutions* (New York: Transnational Publishers, 1991), 368.

[30] For historical development of the problem, see Mwangi wa Githumo, *Land and Nationalism* (Washington, D.C.: University Press of America, 1981).

[31] Benjamin Kiriswa, "African Model of Church as Family: Implications on Ministry and Leadership," *AFER* 43, 3 (June 2001): 99-108, at 102.

[32] Ibid.

[33] Aili Mari Tripp, "Women's Movements, Customary Law, and Land Rights in Africa," *http://www.africa.ufl.edu/asq/v7/v7i4a1.html* (Accessed December 1, 2013). This example is cited from the article entitled "Our Laws Do Not Help Women on Land," *The Monitor, Uganda* (May 6, 2003).

[34] The growing body of evidence from the studies on gender inequality suggests that women's access to land must be given a critical attention in the re-emerging African land rights debate. It is imperative to do so because a household is also an arena where gender-based interests are contested.

[35] United Nations Habitat, "World Urban Forum: Cities without Slums," *United Nations Habitat* (May 2000): 1-15, at 5.

[36] Nyokabi Kamau, Intensify Campaign against Rape," *Daily Nation, Kenya* (February 22, 2003): 9.

[37] Smokin C. Wanjala, *Land Law and Disputes in Kenya* (Nairobi: Oxford University Press, 1990), x.

[38] Janet L. Banda, "Romancing Customary Tenure: Challenges and Prospects for the Neo-Liberal Suitor," in Jeanmarie Fenrich et al., eds., *The Future of African Customary Law* (Cambridge: Cambridge University Press, 2011), 312-336, at 332.

[39] Ibid., 36.

[40] Ibid., 40.

[41] Arthur Okoth Owino, "The State and Public Land," in Ceasar Lukudu et al., *Alienation of Public Land in Kenya* (Nairobi: Catholic University of Eastern Africa, 2000), 22-40, at 38.

[42] Tim Hanstad and Roy Prosterman, "How the Poor Get Washed Away," *The New York Times* (January 14, 2014).

[43] Justice M. Akiwumi, "Report of the Judicial Commission Appointed to Inquire into Tribal Clashes in Rift Valley, Kenya," *Daily Nation, Kenya* (October 19, 2002): 12-26, at 13.

[44] Ahmednasir Andullahi, "Why Judiciary Commission Must Be Reformed Urgently," *Daily Nation, Kenya* (January 19, 2003): 14.

[45] An article analyzing corruption among judges appeared in *The New York Times* one decade ago. To the present there has been no significant change. The article was written by Marc Lacey, "A Crackdown on Corruption in Kenya Snares Judges," *http://www.nytimes.com/2003/10/26/world/a-crackdown-on-corruptionin-kenya-snares-judges.html* (Accessed October 20, 2013).

[46] Akuffo, "The Conception of Land Ownership in African Customary Law and Its Implication for Development," 60.

[47] Ibid., 72

[48] Ibid., 69.

[49] Marcel Rutter, "Land Reform in Africa: Lessons from Kenya," in A. Van Naessen et al., eds., *The Diversity of Development: Essays in Honor of Jan Kleinpenning* (Assen: Van Gorcum, 1997), 71-83, at 79.

[50] Jean-Philippe Platteau, *Land Reform and Structural Adjustment in Sub-Saharan Africa: Controversies and Guidelines* (Rome: Food and Agricultural Organization, Economic and Social Policy Department, 1992), 113.

[51] John Locke examines land ownership under the theme of property. For him, God gave the land to human beings in common for their benefit. He argues that the initiative of improving it to produce wealth is undertaken by individuals, which justifies the ownership. Locke is the most quoted scholar to justify privatization of land rights. For further analysis, see John Locke, *Two Treatises of Government* (New York: Hafner Publishing Company, 1947), 133-146.

[52] Locke's attempt to construct a separation between individual and community, as well as starting from the state of nature to develop a social contract theory could be considered as unrealistic because it is removed from history. His theory on ownership puts emphasis on private ownership at the expense of collective ownership.

[53] Julius Nyerere, "Ujamaa: The Basis of African Socialism," *The Journal of Pan African Studies* 1, 1 (June 1987): 4-11, at 7-8.

[54] The United Nations, Universal Declaration of Human Rights, Article 17.

[55] De Schutter, "How Not to Think of Land-Grabbing: Three Critiques of Large-Scale Investments in Farmland," 269.

[56] Ibid., 268.

[57] For further elaboration, see the analysis of Parselelo Kantai, "In the Grip of the Vampire State: Maasai Land Struggles in

Kenyan Politics," *Journal of Eastern African Studies* 1, 1 (January 2007): 107-122.

[58] Robin Palmer, "The Land Problems in Africa: The Second Scramble," *New People* 54 (June 2002): 13-22, at 14.

[59] Eric Boos, "The Stratifying Effects of Globalization on Tanzanian Culture," *Africa Tomorrow* 2, 2 (June 2002): 119-145, at 120.

[60] Kaj Ahrem, *The Maasai and the State: The Impact of Rural Development Policies on a Pastoral People in Tanzania* (Copenhagen: International Work Group for Indigenous Affairs, 1995), 61.

[61] World Council of Churches, *Land Rights for Indigenous People* (Geneva: World Council of Churches, 1983), 6.

[62] De Schutter, "How Not to Think of Land-Grabbing: Three Critiques of Large-Scale Investments in Farmland," 270.

[63] Ibid.

[64] Ibid.

[65] Obang Metho, U.S. Colleges Accused of African Land Grabs," *http://www.ethiopianreview.com/forum/viewtopic.php?f-2&t-28577* (Accessed July 20, 2013).

[66] De Schutter, "How Not to Think of Land-Grabbing: Three Critiques of Large-Scale Investments in Farmland," 273.

[67] Rasha Warah, "Mining Needs Regulation: Deals with Investors Should be Made Public," *Daily Nation, Kenya* (July 22, 2013): 12.

[68] Lusekelo Philemon, Loliondo Villagers Frustrate Minister Kagasheki Efforts to Vacate for Artelo," *The Guardian, Tanzania* (March 23, 2013): 5.

[69] David Smith, "Tanzania Denies the Plan to Evict Maasai for UAE Royal Hunting Ground," *The Guardian, Tanzania* (August 15, 2012): 4; Tristan McConnell, "Tanzania to Evict Maasai People in Favor of Fee-Paying Trophy Hunters," *http://www.globalpost.com/dispatched/news/regions/africa/130416/tanzan*

ia-maasai-evicted-land-dubai-artello-business (Accessed October 29, 2013).

[70] Ambreena S. Manji, *The Politics of Land Reform in Africa: From Communal Tenure to Free Markets* (London: Zed Books, 2006), 43.

[71] Ibid., 129.

[72] Effective methodologies can reform customary land rights, integration of customary land rights, and statutory land rights do not exist. Legal institutions are more interested in handling scattered cases of land disputes than searching for lasting solutions. Legal researchers are mostly focused on reciting legal codes without reasoning as well as examining the prevailing conditions of life today.

[73] See, for example, the survey of Pauline E. Peters, "Inequality and Social Conflict Over Land in Africa," *Journal of Agrarian Change* 4, 3 (June 2004): 269-314, at 274-275.

[74] Akuffo, "The Conception of Land Ownership in African Customary Law and Its Implication for Development," 77.

[75] Andre Degeorges and Brian Reilly, "Politicization of Land Reform in Zimbabwe: Impacts on Wildlife, Food Production, and the Economy," *International Journal of Environmental Studies* 64, 5 (October 2007): 571-586.

[76] This is precisely the reason that made Robert Mugabe to be re-elected as President of Zimbabwe in 2013, after many years of economic decline and demonization of his regime. People living in rural areas, who are the majority, were more interested in the pledge of regaining the land snatched away from them during the colonial period than the general economic performance of the country.

[77] Bill Derman and Anne Hellum, "Land, Identity, and Violence in Zimbabwe," in Bill Derman et al., eds., *Conflicts Over Land and Water in Africa* (Oxford: Oxford University Press, 2007), 161-186, at 162.

48

[78] Karuti Kanyinga, *Redistribution from Above: The Politics of Land Rights and Squatting on Coastal Kenya* (Uppsala: Nordiska Afrikainstitutet, 2000), 28.

[79] Ibid.

[80] Jean Ensminger, "Changing Property Rights: Reconciling Formal and Informal Rights to Land in Africa," in John N. Drobak and John V.C. Nye, eds., *The Frontiers of the New Institutional Economics* (San Diego: Academic Press, 1907), 165-196, at 183.

[81] African Arguments, "Land Belongs to the Community," *http://www.africanarguments.org/2008/03/11/land-belongs-to-the-community* (Accessed December 22, 2013).

[82] Ibid.

[83] See, for example, the difficulties encountered in attempts of land redistribution in Zimbabwe and Namibia in the article of Pempelani Mufune, "Land Reform Management in Namibia, South Africa, and Zimbabwe: A Comparative Perspective," *International Journal of Rural Management* 6, 1 (June 2010): 1-31, at 3-8, 18-28.

[84] For verification, see the evaluation of Clemente Tabodo Martiale, "Customary Land Ownership Increasingly in Jeopardy: Monitoring Trends in Cameroon," *http://www.presybitarianmission.org/ministries/joininghands/costomatylando wnershipjeopardy* (Accessed October 21, 2013).

[85] Paul Collier, *The Bottom Billion: Why the Poorest Countries are Failing and What Can be Done about It* (Oxford: Oxford University Press, 2007), 96.

[86] Ibid., 180.

[87] Juma Anthony Okuku, "Civil Society and Democratization Processes in Kenya and Uganda: A Comparative Analysis of the Contribution of the Church and NGOs," *South African Journal of Political Studies* 30, 1 (May 2003): 51-63, at 62.

[88] Kanyinga, *Redistribution from Above: The Politics of Land Rights and Squatting on Coastal Kenya*, 7.

[89] Ibid.

[90] Ibid., 9.

[91] Martha Minow, *Between Vengeance and Forgiveness: Facing History after Genocide and Mass Violence* (Boston: Beacon Press, 1998), 5.

Chapter 2

Land, Market, and Morality

The preceding chapter focused on tracing the link between land, identity, and self-determination as a way of establishing the meanings, values, and functions of land. The analysis ensued raised several questions pertaining to the relationship between land rights systems and identity politics. Unfolding the root causes of the increasing land disputes is good, but insufficient to comprehend the scope of the problem under exploration without identifying its implications in other spheres of human experience.

The aim of this chapter is to examine the relationship between land, market, and morality. The discussion begins with a reflection on the market influence on the trend of land-grabbing extended to the relationship between market and morality. This analysis is complimented by an examination of the relationship between privatization, incentive, and efficiency.[1] Suggestions for correcting administrative inefficiency, within public institutions, are given by advancing the ethics of stewardship, management, and accountability.

Market Influence on Land-Grabbing

The trend of land-grabbing mostly exists in urban slums and rural areas endowed with farmland, freshwater, and minerals. This trend is one of the root causes of landlessness, inequality, and conflict. Slum-dwellers, peasants, and pastoralists can easily be evicted from their ancestral-land due to the lack of formal documentation with a well-defined legal procedure of acquisition, ownership, and management.

The root causes of the growing trend of land-grabbing could be situated at two levels, namely, international and national. At the international level, the third world countries have been experiencing a trend of land-grabbing sustained by market forces. The reasons surrounding the trend include the food crisis of the year 2008, which caused a dramatic increase of prices at the international food market.[2] In search for a solution, without delay, the food importing countries produced a strategy of buying land from the third world countries to produce their own food. Several countries, notably the Gulf States, East Asia, and China, have been heavily involved in the venture. The second cause of land-grabbing at the international level is fuel crisis. The rising fuel prices and the diminishing reserves produced reasons for multinational corporations to acquire land for the production of bio-fuel energy as an alternative.[3] These reasons stand out as a driving motive for the trend of land-grabbing in contemporary Africa.

A number of multinational corporations believe that Africa, having vast, arable, and unused land, is appropriate for an agribusiness venture. For them, Africa is viable because land is cheap, and weak institutions and irresponsible leadership make it appropriate for the free market to flourish. These perceptions have opened up a floodgate for foreign investors to acquire land for large-scale farming and oil exploration. Some financial institutions, as a component of the free market system, facilitate the venture. Local leaders, without critical reflection, embrace these strategies thinking that promises of job creation, tax revenue, and infrastructure improvement will automatically bring about rapid economic growth.

Before one could think of the benefits of selling land rights to foreign investors, as a venture for economic development, the following questions must be answered. Are multinational corporations able to bring about economic development to the local population? Are they concerned about the prevailing economic condition of Africa, the condition of underdevelopment, or are they simply doing business? How can we be sure that they are not taking advantage of the weaknesses of the local administration in public institutions? Did people struggle for independence in order to sell ancestral land to foreign corporations and turn the local population into a resource for casual laborers? Is the transfer of land to those who are able to make it productive a guarantee of development for the local population? Is selling land rights a right thing to do in search for economic development? Have people exhausted all possibilities for economic development to the extent of taking the option of selling the most productive land to foreign investors? Is it right to evict indigenous people from their ancestral land in order to accommodate foreign investors? Is rendering indigenous peoples landless, homeless, and unemployed an economic development? These questions may sound provocative, but they are very important.

At the national level, apparently, land-grabbing is generating more insecurity than economic development. The reason is that large quantities of the best agricultural land and fresh water are taken by few individuals for speculation and the resultant economic hardship is progressively creating mistrust among local communities. In urban centers, comparatively, those who are mostly affected are those living in slums. These people are consistently deprived of land rights by state authorities because orders of eviction are secretly approved by political representatives, policymaking bodies, and judicial authorities.[4] The people concerned are not involved in the process of making decisions.

The Ndungu Report, from the perspective of the Kenyan experience, states that "the trend of grabbing the public land provides insights into the struggles over land disputes and corruption in the public institutions."[5] The report says that the established procedures, designed to protect public interest, are perverted to serve private interests. The process is facilitated by patronage, corruption, and secrecy which have seemingly become a part of the African politics. Besides Kenya, other African countries are also experiencing similar cases of displacement, landlessness, and conflict at the grassroots level. It is true, as Joseph Khamisi remarks, that

> The newly installed political class began an orgy of looting, turning government-run institutions into cash-making machines through illegal tendering and outright theft of public funds. The privileged lot turned from being national models of virtue to being megalomaniac with a rapacious appetite for gluttony.[6]

The need for farmland has increased dramatically in recent years because of the growth of the population, environmental degradation, and interest from multinational corporations.

The scramble for land is increasing, not only "because of the scarcity of formal employment and the dependence of the population on the peasantry for survival."[7] Rather, it has also become critical for social status and political competition.

The desire to own land for speculation, on the part of the predatory elite, has fuelled appropriation of the public land reserved for future development. Critics would argue that appropriating parts of the public land has considerably increased due to the decline of the ethics of management and accountability in governance. Under these conditions "land is no longer allocated for development purposes but as a political reward and speculation purposes."[8] Land-grabbing has become a part of the administrative corruption through which the land reserved for public purposes is secretly distributed to politically-connected individuals and multinational corporations. These days we are witnessing a plunder of the public land, whereby land is secretly distributed to individuals for political reasons, leased to foreign corporations, and distributed to friends as gifts.

For African traditions, as we have seen in chapter one, the chief is the only person who has the right to distribute public land. But this trust is no longer reliable because some of those who are entrusted with authority, stewardship, and policymaking responsibilities are not trustworthy persons. The land reserved for future development, including recreation parks, airports, railways, and road expansion is secretly allocated to individuals for personal interest. The widespread abuse of public office affects prospects for economic development. Illegal distribution of the public land is facilitated by the participation of civil servants from the ministries concerned. This phenomenon takes place mostly during the periods of general elections, thereby reinforcing the argument that public land is distributed as a political reward for the purpose of servicing patronage politics. Appropriation of public land for selfish purposes is done by those we trust as guardians of this important national heritage.

These practices have severely affected planning for development. Civil servants, to whom authority of managing common heritage is entrusted, are the root causes of the situation. Corruption and excessive accumulation of wealth, as a sign of institutional decadence, have attracted the ruling class toward land-grabbing. Jacqueline Klopp, from the Kenyan perspective, argues that "irregular allocations of public land to well-connected individuals and land-buying corporations reveal the extent of corruption in public institutions."[9] The dynamics of corruption combines patronage with competition. In this phenomenon, public land becomes a resource for patronage politics. A number of civil servants support the system because of the fear that a change of political regime could limit their privilege of accessing public resources.[10]

The free market, after the fall of communism, has raised unrealistic expectations among people. It promises to bring economic prosperity within a very short time. In the course of time the situation is proving to be the contrary because there are no concrete possibilities on the ground. Effects of land-grabbing include displacement of the vulnerable people, food production for the international market, and the destruction of the peasantry. On the same note the experience shows that environmental destruction, repression of the grassroots communities, forced migration, and inequality are increasing.[11] The forgotten wisdom is that economic development is a process, not an event. Public officials have already embraced the venture without serious reflection. With the triumph of the free market in the last two decades there are important conversations that have been forgotten, including wealth and poverty, fairness and justice, private and public interests, and authority and accountability. The next section examines the relationship between market and morality as an attempt to capture the complexity and scope underlying land disputes.

Market and Morality

Before we embark on the task of examining the relationship between market and morality it is appropriate to establish the link between economics and morality. This platform would help us to find out how market and morality relate in actual life. This presentation makes reference to the studies undertaken by Amartya Sen, Philip Wogaman, Michael Sandel, and Christian Conrad on the relationship between economics and morality as a way of enriching the discussion.[12]

The account of Sen on the relationship between ethics and economics illuminates considerably the origin of the problem we are about to address and it could be the best way to begin the discussion.[13] His arguments rest upon the premise that "economics must pay attention to the ethical considerations that shape human behavior and judgment."[14] For him, studies of economics could be enriched by paying attention to the studies of ethics, which, "in turn, can benefit from a closer contact with economics."[15] Many scholars think that studies of economics do not need attributes of friendliness and goodwill. For them, economics is about money, property, production, labor, market, and profit, not about feelings and emotions.

For Sen, modern studies in economics are impoverished by the distance grown between itself and ethics.[16] The reason is that they are confined in statistics with a strong tendency to ignore the import of ethics. They operate within a "format of a narrowly construed non-ethical view of human motivation and behavior."[17] Some ethicists, on the other hand, are confined within a framework removed from historical experience. These two extremes keep morality and economics apart. John Milbank, in view of challenging ahistorical approaches, argues that an ethical analysis removed from historical experience is problematic and empty of content.[18] Ethics cannot be separated from cultural, political, and economic experiences. For it to become reasonable its dynamics must be attached to the experiences and interpretations of history. There cannot be a historically-founded ethical analysis without mediation of historical narratives.

Any attempt dealing with economic relations must acknowledge that human behavior plays a significant role in socio-economic life. For Sen,

> The study of economics, though related immediately to the pursuit of wealth, is at a deeper level linked up with other studies, involving the assessment and enhancement of fundamental values. The neglect of the ethical analysis of sentiments and behavior fits well into the distancing of economics from ethics.[19]

The tendency of separating economics and morality is increasingly creating unnecessary conflict of values.

Turning to the relationship between market and morality it is interesting to note that the politics of the free market complains about "bureaucratic barriers and other restrictions imposed on economic transactions that make trade difficult and hamper production."[20] Proponents of the free market, according to Wogaman, argue that

> Nobody should attempt to set priorities for the whole society. If each of us will just look after oneself, that will yield the best results for society as a whole. The free market does what no individual or group could hope to do. It motivates everybody to contribute their best efforts, because otherwise they will not have anything to exchange. But it leaves everybody free to exchange what they have for whatever they want, thereby assuring that the greatest good will result by invisible hand.[21]

For them, poverty is a natural condition that individuals have to deal with by themselves, while wealth is a creative action of free individuals acting under the discipline of the free market system. The state should not be allowed to intervene in the processes of the wealth creation and distribution. Intervention of the state is an obstruction toward efficiency. If this is the case, then can we afford to leave land distribution, ownership, and management to the free market operating under the doctrine of laissez-faire? What guarantee do we have that can make us trust free market? To strengthen the claims of freedom and individualism, proponents of the free market argue that

> Where people are not accorded freedom to make their own choices and to live with the consequences of those choices they are generally made into the instruments of somebody else's choosing. We may think we are doing people a favor by solving all their problems for them. Actually we are treating them as less than

human beings and undermining their own self-respect and creative potential.[22]

The distribution of goods and delivery of services should not be the duty of the state. This way of thinking presents personal freedom and self-interest as virtues.

Those who support the free market believe that "nobody should worry about what the economy is doing as a whole. A free market economy takes care of itself. Social change should be left to occur naturally."[23] These ideas have become the foundation of the doctrine of the free market, social contact, and privatization.[24] The role of the state should not include distribution of goods and delivery of services. On this account theories that support the free market persuade people to believe that the responsibility of making moral judgments must be left to the free market. This way of thinking has already hijacked healthcare programs, land management systems, labor laws, and market prices.

Others believe that the free market is neutral in the way it functions to balance supply and demand. But experience shows that unfettered market does not respect collective interests such as preservation of the environment, rights of small-scale farmers, and decent wage for laborers. Land, from the market viewpoint, is seen as a matter to be exploited to satisfy the needs of human beings. The right to own land as well as determine its usage depends upon the financial status of the person involved in the transaction.[25]

The free market, as an exchange of goods that promotes freedom of choice, autonomy, and creativity as a means to increase productivity, strongly advances the notions of commoditization and commercialization of non-market goods. The meaning of land, as I have demonstrated in chapter one, is tied to social relations. The economic function is only one of many functions of land. So, to make the value of land completely dependent on the market value would be to subordinate everything to the value of the market.

Claims of commoditization and commercialization of land have somehow distorted the meaning of land. Commoditization is the process by which land becomes an economic commodity controlled by market forces. The situation generates four points of contention: first, land has both economic value and social value; second, land has economic value, but it cannot be limited to economic value only; third, the commoditization of land has ultimately made its market value replace its social value; and fourth, market value can actually replace social value. The claim of commoditization generates significant risk because it advocates commercialization, monopolization, and greed.

To a certain extent, claims of commoditization and commercialization of land have weakened protective measures toward public land and, as a result, trust has been anchored on the self-regulation of the market. The value of land differs from other forms of commodities because it accommodates a wider spectrum of human experience. From the perspective of the market, the value of the land is measured in terms of how much could be generated from it. But in reality the value of land is not limited to the quality a developer places on it. Rather, its value is extended to the entire life of the universe it sustains. Destruction of traditional ethical systems without replacing them with a functional alternative has led to the disintegration of traditional value systems. With an attitude that adores the market, the poor, the land, water, and forests could be reduced to whatever value the market ascribes to them. The free market presents land as a commodity to be traded for profit. For traditional communities, land, rivers, forests, and lakes are much more than a means of production. They are the foundation of a culture that facilitates social, political, cultural, and spiritual functions.

The view of land as something that has an economic value only is common in materialistic cultures. For African traditions, clearly, the value of land is not only the added quality a developer places on it because it is extended to the multiple dimensions of human experience. Land cannot be priced following the rationale of the free market because its value is more than a commodity that could be traded.

The value of land cannot be measured by the amount of profit it can generate and what can be extracted from it. It cannot be equated to the temporary interest a developer places on it. Rather, its value permeates permanently in all dimensions of human life. It cannot be priced, commercialized, or sold at a market price because its value is more than a commodity that can be calculated arithmetically. Land is more than a market commodity because of its multidimensional possibilities of meaning, value, and function. There must be a way of seeing morality as an embodiment of economics while at the same time making a distinction between economics and morality without building a wall of separation between them. The key point is that the material dimension is necessarily connected to the non-material dimension.

It is inappropriate to apply the argument of willing-buyer and willing-seller, which is based on the assumption that everything can be marketed. Certain categories of goods cannot be considered to have values with market equivalences. The value of land belongs to a moral category of goods for which an equivalent market value cannot be established. The non-market values are critical to the land debate because certain goods cannot be marketed. The market tends to ignore values which are considered "impossible to render the equivalence in commercial terms."[26] If land has a sacred dimension, then it cannot be traded as other goods. The multiple meanings, values, and functions of land, as I have mentioned earlier, mediate the sacred dimension that cannot be displayed on the market. But the free market attempts to confine the value of land within the sphere of economics. It appeals to the influence of the market as a force that can persuade people to believe that the value of land is exclusively determined by the free market, and as such land should only be perceived from the standpoint of production, market, and profit.

A number of liberal thinkers take very lightly the claims of the collective rights. They put an exaggerated emphasis on freedom, privatization, and market. Rights are perceived as legal entities with instrumental use rather than moral values. For them, the function of land is entirely premised on economic anthropology. Following the same reasoning, their theories on economics have no place for psychology, spirituality, and morality. These approaches have ultimately become the foundation of the modern principles of economics.

Wogaman, in view of challenging the free market, argues that "economics touches all aspects of life. It cannot be trusted to take care of itself, and it is far too important to turn over to professionals alone. Economics cut adrift from the values that give direction to the human venture."[27] The assumption of laissez-faire removes economics from decision-making process and the public interest because it advocates fragmentation of the human spirit. There is an intrinsic link between economics and morality. Morality, as a conception of the good, actualizes economics in social relations.

The problem that must be addressed entails an understanding of values that transcend the material value. To certain circumstances it is not clear whether we should favor the free market system or state-controlled market system.[28] The point of contention is that the market alone cannot do everything to satisfy all human needs. The art of balancing institutional functions is crucial for understanding human life in society. Economic values do not necessarily contradict the goal of moral values.

Turning to the weaknesses of the market we can say that, in the way it operates, free market undermines the social nature of human beings. The intrusion of the market could be interpreted as a lack of disciplined efficiency and obstruction to other spheres of human experience. The free market becomes intrusive when moral decisions are determined by its forces. Those who have resources in the form of wealth, ownership, and authority are likely to be the people who decide how those same resources should be distributed, and they are likely to do so while favoring their own interests.

One would be naïve to think that the free market does not need morality. The reason is that, as Conrad points out,

> Absolutely efficient markets are impossible because the actors in the markets are human beings. Humans are fallible. They are emotional and imperfect and do not always act efficiently or rationally. Even if humans strive to attain perfection or occasionally claim to be perfect or have god-like control over nature, they are not.[29]

The preceding statement affirms that the market is a human institution with its weaknesses. For instance, the bankruptcies of the banks and companies which caused the world economic crisis that has lasted since 2008 were caused by unnecessary risks and unethical behaviors undertaken in search of short-term advantages. The limitless enrichment of a few people is usually undertaken at the expense of those who are vulnerable.

The scope of the free market is thus limited because it undermines collective values.[30] The reason is that if we assign an overarching role to the market, which puts an excessive emphasis on the pursuit of self-interest, it could be unbalanced and destructive. The challenges we encounter under the free market, operating under the doctrine of laissez-faire, include excesses of selfishness and greed. These conditions cause extreme suffering for those who are vulnerable. An unchallenged market, argues Robert Skidelsky, "converts avarice, greed, and envy into virtues."[31] For him, the free market lacks the principle of justice, and to correct the situation "justice, in exchange, must be supplied from outside the market."[32] The principle of justice focuses on the search for a balance between extremes, thereby making rights and duties two faces of the same coin because they complement each other.

According to Sandel, "the logic of buying and selling no longer applies to material goods alone but increasingly governs the whole life. It is time to ask whether we want to live this way."[33] The market, boldly speaking, has come to govern all spheres of human experience. There is a strong belief that the market holds the key for freedom and prosperity. Can the market be a primary means to achieve the public good? The world's financial crisis of the year 2008 shows that the market, without moral consideration, is defective.

Because of greed, the ethical demands of responsibility and accountability are ignored. On this matter, argues Sandel, "the root cause arises from the fact that there is expansion of markets into spheres where they don't belong."[34] There is a need to evaluate the role that the market should play in the public sphere. He continues to argue that we need a public debate about how should the "markets operate and what it means to keep markets in their place. To have this debate we need to think through the moral limits of markets. We need to ask whether there are some things money should not buy."[35] For him, there are things that money cannot buy, including moral values.

Land, following the rationale of the market, has been turned into a market commodity. But, as Sandel correctly remarks,

> Markets do not only allocate goods; they also express and promote certain attitudes toward the goods being exchanged. Market values crowd out moral values and virtues that have no economic utility. When we decide that certain goods may be bought and sold, we decide at least implicitly, that it is appropriate to treat them as commodities, as instruments of profit and use. But not all goods are valued in this way.[36]

Caution is required because we can easily relegate moral values to the whims of the market. At this point we have to ask ourselves these questions: what are the limits of markets? What role should the market play in social relations and policymaking procedures? Which criteria should we use to make a distinction between goods that could be traded and goods that cannot be traded? How can we distinguish market values from non-market values taking into account the fact that the two are closely interrelated? These questions raise a great deal of difficulty for any attempt to identify and propose limitations of the market.

Meanwhile, observes Sandel, "there is a lack of reasoned public participation in the public discourse because important questions are not asked. People tend to leave their moral and spiritual convictions behind when they enter the public square."[37] And as a result the dynamics of the free market takes advantage of the situation by emptying the public sphere of moral reasoning, thereby resulting into impoverishment of the public sphere. If people are reluctant to freely engage in moral and spiritual arguments in the public discourse, then the free market takes over the public sphere. Subsequently, it uses the opportunity to make decisions for everything. The failure to limit the reach of the market has considerably weakened the public discourse. The market has taken over the lives of the people insofar as it makes decisions that reduce people to material goods that can be marketed. The situation calls us to examine the role of the market in social relations, public discourse, and public institutions.

Sandel points out that there is a "growing reach of the market into spheres of life governed by non-market norms. Many people would claim that people should be free to buy and sell whatever they please, as long as they don't violate anyone's rights."[38] This way of thinking allows people to do whatever they want irrespective of moral obligations. For example, the free market has gone as far as buying and selling human organs. The consumer is not interested to know the origin of the organ that is being bought even if it was acquired by murdering another person. It is apparent that the free market has become wild and the public has somehow refrained from challenging extreme ways of thinking and acting. What matters most is the end result, not the means used to arrive at the result. Those who are affected by the means used are the vulnerable people. In this case, clearly, those who benefit from the transaction are those standing at the end of the chain as suppliers or consumers. Those who are found in the middle pay the price. This means negative consequences hurt those who are vulnerable, not those who are standing at the two ends of the transaction, the supplier and the consumer.

These arguments could be summed up as follows: first, corruption corrodes moral life; second, the free market does not consider the means used to obtain the required goods for the market; third, the well-being of those who are found in the middle of the process of production is nobody's business; and fourth, destructive possibilities prevail because these ways of thinking and making judgment are not challenged. Following the rationale of the free market, the rich are those who stand at the two ends, either as suppliers or as consumers.

For those at the ends of the chain, the suffering of those caught in between does not matter. The claim of willing-seller and willing-buyer, without considering other values at stake, could be considered as an attempt to avoid moral responsibility. The claim that the people involved do everything willingly cannot be justified because those who suffer the consequences have no ability to escape. "The market favors those who have financial capacity because goods are allocated based on the ability and willingness to pay."[39] Abstract economic reasoning could deceive us because it shows that everything is alright. Those who are at the ends have money, power, and privilege. The much heralded theory of trickle-down effect does not really function in actual life.

The claim of willing-seller and willing-buyer represents a movement of neo-colonization. It is an imposed ideology because local people are literally evicted from their lands and forced to accept whatever meagre compensation that is determined between the government and companies concerned, creating a situation of unwilling-seller and willing-buyer. Examples that can demonstrate the argument are found in southern Tanzania and northern Uganda.

I concur with Sandel that certain things are not for sale. Market forces encourage people to prioritize material goods, and the privileged do it unconsciously. In recent years, the market-oriented way of thinking has permeated even the "spheres of life traditionally governed by non-market norms."[40] This obviously happens when the dynamics of the free market crowd out non-market values and thereby undermine the place of moral values in social relations. This is evident because the role of decision-making has passed from the people affected by those decisions to supposedly non-human corporations and markets.

There are values that cannot be obtained at a market price. We can only get them through the practice of virtues. To justify this argument, Sandel claims that "there is a sharp distinction between two kinds of goods: the things money can't buy, and the things money can buy."[41] One could say that buying exams cannot make a person worthy of the knowledge signified by the certificate one holds. The person concerned would discover that knowledge entails self-cultivation because the one concerned will be unable to do what the certificate certifies. The approach of using market value to dominate other spheres diminishes the dimension of moral values. Converting land into a market commodity does not completely destroy the meaning of land, but it diminishes the way it is perceived. Presenting land in the free market in search for a market value could diminish the esteemed perception that land deserves. It is unrealistic to think that the market alone can overcome all social problems.[42]

We can sum up the limitations of the free market in six ways: first, "market exchanges are not always as voluntary as proponents of the free market think; second, the corruption involved leads to the degrading effect to the non-market goods;"[43] third, the so-called freedom of choice is questionable because there could be latent forces of influence within the person exercising the freedom of choice; fourth, some choices are not truly voluntary because they depend on the conditions surrounding the person making the choice; fifth, market transactions degrade moral values, because market transactions diminish the value of the goods beings exchanged; sixth, the free market incentives could be interpreted as inducement for corruption rather than a motivation to increase efficiency.

From the standpoint of Sandel, "introducing money into a non-market setting can change people's attitudes and crowd out moral values and civic commitment."[44] The defective effect of the financial incentive lessens people's commitment toward the good that could lead to the loss of the sense of civic duty. Feelings, motivations, friendliness, good will, and service to others are in fact genuine determinants of efficiency. With reliance on the market to control public decisions, there could be no possibility to eradicate corruption because it is governed by excess self-interest, profit, and greed. We need other institutions that can balance the forces of the market. But if the opposite persists, then extreme forms of the free market would thrive. A balanced way of proceeding is required to avoid the possibility of substituting morality with self-interest. The extension of the market "into every sphere of life, including those traditionally governed by non-market value, obscure the life of virtues."[45] We should not allow the market to take over all spheres of life because the market cannot buy moral values. Land is one of the goods that money cannot buy. Consequently, we cannot leave the task of making moral judgment to the free market.

Concerning the relationship between the market and morality we can say, as Sen, Wogaman, Sandel, and Conrad attest, that economics and markets cannot be separated from social relations because different dimensions of human experience complement one another. Removing economics from moral discourse would impoverish economics. It is just the same as separating moral discourse from historical experience, including economics, would impoverish morality. Moral discourse must bring together metaphysical and empirical dimensions of human experience. Life becomes distorted when non-material values are perceived as though they were material values.

Each dimension of human experience is distinct; however, it cannot be separated from the whole, neither as intrinsic good nor instrumental good. None of them can be treated as the end-in-itself. Instrumental values are useful for the realization of intrinsic values. Instrumental and intrinsic dimensions of morality are inextricably tied together. It is true that we need the market. But market alone cannot give us everything we need to organize human life in a reasonable way. We also need the role of other institutions.

The free market, because of the over-emphasis on self-interest and profit, can easily undermine the life of virtues. The situation suggests that institutions that can regulate the role of the market in a balanced way are indispensable. The market is a very powerful force for development, but the challenge is how to make it promote both material and non-market values. The market needs not only the proceeds of the material values, but also moral values so as to transcend excesses generated by the doctrine of laissez-faire.[46] Such a balance will make it serve the public good instead of serving few individuals at the expense of the multitude.

The dynamics of the market motivate human ingenuity to maximize wealth creation. They do it by guaranteeing freedom of choice, innovation, and incentive. In this engagement human creativity is unleashed to benefit humanity. But extreme tendencies of the market could be destructive. It is right to allow market forces to operate, but not to the extent of allowing them to make moral judgments. The market is a two-edged sword: it could be either constructive or destructive depending on how we approach it. The introduction of the free market where there is rule of law and public order can improve economic life. But where it operates without institutional supervision and surveillance it could suppress collective values with a possibility of replacing them with profit-oriented enterprises. For example, selling land rights is an extreme form of the free market that requires institutional adjustment. Market and morality should influence one another and the separation between them should be regarded as a misconception of how public institutions operate in human society. Others would argue that morality influences the goods we buy and investments we make, meaning that moral values inform market attitudes. The discourse on the market cannot remain confined within the claims of self-interest, production, and efficiency. It requires an import from morality in order to be balanced, efficient, and beneficial to all. Moral values are foundational to market economy.

The market is useful on condition that it facilitates exchange of goods, motivates factors that increase efficiency, and reinforces quality assurance. It generates conditions necessary to balance supply and demand through price regulation. But the market is by no means self-sufficient, inclusive, or perfect.[47] The claim that the market is self-sufficient cannot be justified. The free market alone cannot solve all human problems because its reach is limited.[48] In well-ordered societies, the exercise of power is strongly moderated by institutional interactions.

A well-ordered economic system is a balanced system whose equilibrium results from the balance of institutional interaction. The diversity of institutions increases capacity toward mutual-support rather than isolation.[49] This argument is significant because in the process of establishing and maintaining a balance of power one institution cannot substitute another since each one is supreme in its proper sphere of influence, has its own distinctive contribution to the social whole, and needs contribution from the other institutions.

Privatization, Incentive, and Efficiency

Is privatization of inefficient state agencies a wise decision? Many governments aim at attaining efficiency by delegating its responsibilities to private firms through auction systems. It is widely believed that privatization would increase efficiency and production. But there is no guarantee that delegation of public duties to private firms will always succeed. Weaknesses of privatization, combined with emerging ways of how to organize a private firm to maximize profit, in which investors are free to move the capital and profit whenever and wherever they want, could result in structural inequality, a situation that could devastate the vulnerable section of the population.

The lack of effective public institutions leaves room for defective forms of privatization to thrive. Multinational corporations exploit administrative weakness within public institutions by giving incomplete information in contracts, bribing authorities concerned so as to override existing legal procedures and maximize profit by evading taxation. For example, the multinational corporations mining in Tanzania are exempted from taxation for a period of five years.[50] Some contracts give very small royalty to the government to the extent that the mining venture becomes synonymous to the act of looting. Obviously, these types of contracts will not result into economic development. The same approach has been applied to the existing practice of granting land to foreign investors. Secrecy and corruption surrounding public contracts and land allocation reveal the lack of transparency and accountability.

Proponents of privatization, however, argue that competition is good for improving the quality of goods, efficiency of the producer, and services. "Producers compete with each other to serve people in an excellent way. This is not a dog eat dog situation, but rather a system that incentivizes service to others."[51] Efficiency enhances separation of the state from the enterprises owned by individuals. This arrangement pressurizes each individual to produce wealth so as to survive, and consequently the state is freed from the burden of caring for individuals. According to Richard Coughling,

> Private and profit-seeking organizations perform with greater efficiency than public organizations. This observation turns out to be true. Empirical studies comparing public and private performance in comparable activities identify a private advantage in simple efficiency, albeit with some significant exceptions and conditions.[52]

It is clear that privately-owned enterprises are more efficient than public agencies. Efficiency and quality are found with private enterprises. Others, according to Wogaman, claim that

> Private firms operate closer to optimal cycle. Their work rules are more flexible, and hiring and procurement are less rule-bound. Innovation is more rapid, machines are more up-to-date, less money is spent on hiring employees, and more on equipping them. Employee incentives and sanctions are subtler and more effective. On the contrary, government agencies are structured to guarantee procedural fairness, openness, and accountability. But both theory and evidence identify only a potential private advantage in efficiency.[53]

Where competition is weak there is limited success. With private enterprises there is supervised performance, quality assurance, and competition intended to increase production.

Advantages of privatization could be summed up in five ways. First, it is true that privatization, through incentive, motivates creativity as a means of increasing production and quality. Second, it is a resource that enhances economic enticement and quality by displaying better managerial skills and creative potential to increase production. Third, it is a tool for reforming public agencies functioning without a clear mission, motivation, and quality. Fourth, incentives motivate individuals to be efficient, productive, and creative. Fifth, it corrects the lack of competitive edge among employees while providing better services to the customer as well as improving the infrastructure.

Are incentives geared to encouraging performance or to manipulating those who give service? Market incentives, apparently, have been understood as a way of promoting selfishness and individualism. Incentives are somehow perceived or interpreted as bribes. In certain circumstances and contexts, financial incentives undermine moral demands and, as such, they could be interpreted as bribes. This is because the claim of an incentive puts more emphasis on self-interest than on public interest.

Can we use private enterprises as a means to serve public ends? Privatization requires institutions that can oversee the entire process of wealth creation so as to protect public interest. Many people believe that public services offered through "civil service organizations reinforce communal character, while the profit-oriented enterprises would pollute it."[54] Arguments given by several observers reveal that private enterprises are confined to the intention of making profit. In recent years, we have been relying upon the free market to think as well as make decisions for us. Moral responsibility is at stake when the state delegates its responsibility to the profit-oriented enterprises to undertake certain duties for the benefit of the public without proper supervision.

Ineptitudes of the public institutions cannot be corrected by private organizations. Hiring private companies to be delegates for public institutions could be interpreted as a sign of weakness. Corruption finds its ground in contracts between the private companies and the public institutions because the process of writing contracts requires foresight and imagination. In some cases, government representatives engaged in contract-writing and bidding lack imagination and integrity. They can neither interpret the contracts nor search for alternative ways of thinking. Moreover, there is no guarantee that corporations, without institutional supervision, will excel in implementing public projects. It is not my intention to undermine the role of private enterprises; however, it is evident that privatization is limited and, as such, we need other institutions that can play the role of safeguarding public interest.

Despite the benefits privatization brings, its focus on self-interest and maximization of profit makes it vulnerable to greed. Weaknesses of privatization could be summed up in seven categories: first, the uncontrolled urge to maximize profit tends to disregard public objectives and moral values; second, the profit-oriented tendency goes together with the lack of transparency and accountability that supports the momentum for corruption; third, inflation is increased by unjustifiably raised prices; fourth, there is room for the avoidance of taxation; fifth, there is absolute separation of the private sphere from the public sphere; sixth, privatization, assisted by the growth of the free market and without control from public institutions, could result in loss of control over public land as well as the lands belonging to the vulnerable individuals and communities; and, seventh, accumulation through landholding could facilitate processes of exclusion, class formation, and inequality. These weaknesses show that privatization is a limited system. The so-called incentive could thus be interpreted as a form of corruption.

Comparatively, privatization is successful in the West because public institutions that play the role of safeguarding public interest are efficient. The failure in the less-developed countries, argues Hernando De Soto, arises from the lack of commonly-accepted land rights systems and inability to convert labor into capital.[55] In order to comprehend the limitation of privatization, the following analysis will focus on the causes of corruption and on how it has become increasingly linked to excessive self-interest as a motive for privatization.

What are the causes of corruption? Can we eradicate corruption from public institutions? Corruption could be defined as an abuse of public office in order to advance private interest.[56] It has many forms, and the way it is practiced vary from one context to another. Corruption, as a symptom of structural disorganization and inequality, could also be described as an abuse of the power that has been entrusted to the officials presiding over public institutions. It includes the vices of fraud, bribery, and manipulation of the established ethical conduct and legal standard. Bribery is not limited to financial incentives alone; it is also given in non-financial forms.

Petty corruption is practiced to solicit public services. Those who give this type of bribe are the poor. They give bribe to civil servants in order to receive public services that are, in fact, their right to receive freely. Large-scale corruption is practiced to manipulate the public order. This form of corruption takes place in governmental contracts, taxation, tenders, and selling of public goods. It degrades the efficiency of the public institutions that are designed to render public services, since there are public funds already set aside for these services. Conditions that make corruption a means to get services are deliberately created by those who want to maximize their income at the expense of those who are seeking public services.

Causes of corruption include unequal distribution of wealth, patronage politics, underpaid civil servants, and greed. Effects of corruption include inefficiency of public institutions, loss of tax revenues, and dilapidated public infrastructure. Corruption is a symptom of mismanagement, inefficiency, and over-centralization of decision-making processes. We need structures of governance that can challenge the widespread tendency of embezzling public funds. The problem arises from the tendency to put self-interest above the common good. Corruption has become a formidable obstacle to poverty eradication. It exists in every country and has become a part of governance and leadership. This situation persists because of the weak institutions, excessive bureaucracy, and underpaid civil servants. It is found in public service, resource distribution, and investment procedure.

Analyses of management and corruption are paramount for the understanding of contemporary African politics. Land management is largely obstructed by forms of governance characterized by inefficiency. Corruption undermines rights-claims when what matters is the preferential treatment of relatives, friends, and cronies. Institutionalized corruption favors status quo and patronage politics.

Institutionalized corruption has largely hampered economic development. Eradication of corruption is thus a genuine way to secure natural resources for the well-being of the majority. It is true that a number of civil servants have turned themselves into thieves in the way they govern public institutions. The current forms of governance and leadership have, to a large extent, eroded public trust and confidence.

Large-scale corruption compromises development efforts despite the political measures adopted in order to address the situation. In the end, it is possible to eliminate corruption through the setting up of a strict code of ethics that can oversee the processes of governance and leadership. An ethics commission can help people to know their rights and duties. People would have to learn to be strict with the leaders they have elected. Rules and anti-corruption commissions may be multiplied, but, without moral formation, corruption will prevail.

As already pointed out, there are several causes of corruption. It thrives where power is centralized in the hands of a few individuals who control decision-making processes. The practice is possible where there is monopoly over information and lack of structured procedures, transparency, and accountability. Corruption is usually shrouded in dictatorial leadership. According to John Powelson,

When power is concentrated in one or few focal points, corruption pays off for the powerful, since no one can check them. As rival political figures arise with the power each one sees an advantage to curbing the corruption of the others. When any given power holder is but one of many, one's gain from one's own corruption is small relative to the loss from the corruption of the others.[57]

This means corruption, from the higher ranks of administration, can be eradicated through devolution of power, while at the grassroots it could be addressed by delegating services. At the middle, where civil servants control service delivery, bureaucracy gives rise to the culture of corruption. Powelson argues that lack of clarity on the part of "bureaucratic regulations offers all sorts of opportunities for graft on the part of officials, and fraud on the part of would-be beneficiaries, in search of a handout without entitlement to it."[58]

The anti-corruption laws are sometimes enacted as a means to get rid of political opponents.[59] When those in positions of authority propose anti-corruption campaigns, they do so for show because they have no intention of implementing any resolution. It is not clear whether these initiatives of "calling to remove corrupt leaders mark an incipient public rage against corruption or whether they are strategies intended to eliminate political opponents."[60] Corruption is often caused by the lack of clarity in administrative positions. In patronage systems there is no clear separation of private and public powers, and those in authority may treat public authority as a means of maximizing private interest. Mixing private interest with that of the public is a condition deliberately created to generate confusion that enables corruption to thrive. When power is concentrated in one person possibilities of abuse are higher. So, the "main virtue of the moral economy lies in its cultural acceptance that neither power nor wealth may be concentrated anywhere, either in government or in private corporations."[61] It is difficult to distinguish a gift from an incentive intended to be a motivation or a bribe.

The challenges raised here can only be thoroughly addressed through common effort, shared responsibility, and determined commitment. Success in eradicating corruption is neither automatic nor dependent on the multiplication of rules; rather, it is attained by interiorizing civic obligations that are focused on the process of shaping public institutions and promoting civic virtues. Although national constitutions contain progressive provisions for the ethics of stewardship, transparency, and accountability for good governance, the challenge of wiping out corruption requires more than all that. It further requires institutions that promote long-term formation of the citizens. Character is not formed at once. It is a process of human growth and of the appropriation of values.

The corruption of land management occurs when the patronage politics use common resources to bribe voters in order to win elections. In search of votes, for example, those vying for positions of leadership buy supporters by offering them different forms of inducements. This is a widespread practice in contemporary Africa. In part, this system generates corruption with many candidates "turning to alternative sources of patronage, including public lands."[62] The struggle to identify illegal allocations of public land is a challenge because the secrecy of the patrimonial politics does not allow people to question leaders on the source of their wealth. A letter of the Southern African Catholic Bishops Conference argues that "bribery, collusion, and all other forms of corruption thrive in conditions of secrecy and concealment, and they persist because people allow them to continue. When bribery becomes a way of life for civil servants, business people, or church personnel, their real responsibilities are put aside in pursuit of making money for themselves."[63]

Privatization, as it applies to the free market, is limited. It is true that privatization could boost the economy for the reasons I have already mentioned. But such a success will not be possible without due attention to the formation of strong institutions that are built on the principles of efficiency in taxation, integrity in civil service, and accountability to the public. These conditions can be realized if there is a decentralized system of governance.

Many argue that corruption in public institutions cannot be eradicated. For them, public institutions lack motivation, ambition, competition, and incentive. The argument given is that corruption is rampant where there is insecurity. Public institutions are tied to collective decisions which take a long time to come by because of bureaucracy and inefficiency, while private enterprises use a much simpler mechanism. Corrupt officials find a way to appropriate public funds allocated to the programs with the use of money that cannot be verified easily.

People give bribe to get public services they freely deserve because they are ignorant of procedures, rights, and laws. A long-term approach to curb corruption would have to focus on cultivating civic virtues, which include prudence, service, responsibility, and justice geared toward the common good. This could be done by introducing children to the ethics of civic responsibility and the common good right from the early years. A number of higher learning institutions, however, tend to ignore studies that promote civic virtues, especially philosophy, theology, literature, spirituality, and ethics. Such studies are widely perceived as superfluous. A number of scholars think that public life does not need spirituality or morality. But the truth is that formation in morality is crucial for socio-economic development because it introduces people to the concepts of right and wrong. We cannot expect people to lead a life of virtues, deliver community service, or have a sense of public accountability if they have not received this kind of formation.

Some academic institutions neglect moral formation perhaps because of ignorance. Studies in social justice, human rights, theological ethics, and religious education are often excluded from the curricula. Many universities do not have faculties of theology, religious studies, ethics, or philosophy. An all-round, well-balanced, and integrated academic formation is achieved when academic institutions are value-oriented, not only market-oriented.[64] The contrary is an academic training that produces graduates with a science but without conscience. The situation is compounded by a skewed understanding, organization and delivery of academic formation, which creates a framework that does not consider moral formation as an important aspect of public life and, therefore, a responsibility of academic institutions.

Training for moral values is portrayed as a less important dimension in academic formation.[65] But, in reality, moral values are the most important components of a socio-economic organization that is characterized by efficiency, integrity, and accountability. We cannot talk of good governance and responsible leadership without making reference to moral values. Socio-economic development emanates from this foundation. Practical wisdom teaches that good governance cannot be achieved by people who lack moral values.[66] Those who govern public institutions are expected to be morally upright people.

There are different ways that could be used to overcome corruption. They could be summed up in two categories, namely, managerial supervision and character formation. Formation of the mind and the heart entails shaping the character. It is a process that enables individuals to infuse daily life with moral values, consequently enabling them to distance themselves from inappropriate conduct. It requires examination of one's actions and the effects those actions have on the lives of other people. If we are to succeed we have to make education, both formal and informal, a means of training the mind and the heart, especially of the youth, so that we can have responsible citizens. Morally speaking, formation in civic virtues should be the foundation of academic formation. As Maulana Wahiddudin points out,

> Formation in virtues makes one evaluate actions in terms of their results, a major factor in having a sense of responsibility. One who cultivates such a perspective is able to see things in terms of value. It helps to keep emotions under control and brings peace of mind. An education system that includes [moral and] spiritual values in instruction will help students imbibe eternal values and truths that enable them to not only develop their intellectual capacity but also fulfill their role as responsible human beings in society.[67]

Academic formation must include the task of training people to become duty-conscious and responsible members of society.

Excessive aspiration for self-enrichment among administrators plays a key role in bringing about economic crisis. "People are influenced in their behavior by their view of the world. And moral values must be shown by example and included in education."[68] True education is based on the ability to serve the community. Clearly, to mould this ability, "one needs much more than a professional education, one needs instruction in history, philosophy, literature, theology, and logic."[69] A lack of such moral formation and a disintegration of moral traditions have resulted in the rise of irresponsible leadership and inefficient governance in public institutions. A value system is weakened when "it is no longer practiced. For this reason there is a need to educate children and socialize members of a society in all areas."[70] If this formation does not take place negative effects will be felt in all areas of public life. Moral formation of the youth needs role models, insertion into practice, and morally-informed education. Without this dimension the idea of the common good will be lacking in the public sphere.

For a society to flourish there must be a healthy political culture promoted by the cultivation of civic virtues. This objective can be achieved through moral formation and building of stronger systems of accountability and management. In this way, governance is strengthened. The tendency to use common resources in ways that aggravate inequalities, a situation that stimulates resentments among those who do not benefit from it and thereby leading to conflict, is thus eliminated. For a long a long-term solution, institutions which are focused on formation must include moral education to empower people with the spirit of responsibility, accountability, and service. They have to encourage them to cherish, love, and cultivate civic virtues. The positive results of this kind of training will be revealed at the level of civic responsibility, especially by those who are given the responsibility of stewardship, leadership, and enforcement of the law.

Civic virtues, like freedom for excellence, set the ground for public life. They invite people to seek goodness by setting standards of discerning what is good for the community. They nurture the character of civic responsibility that emerges from the human heart toward the quest for happiness. Weakness in management organization arises when those in position of authority think that they are dispensed from observing the required moral standards. Excesses of self-interest overshadow the life of virtue, the life that calls us to serve others. Selfishness reveals itself in the public sphere when a person sees everything from the perspective of self-interest.

Formation in civic virtues, as a process of infusing moral values in social action, offers an opportunity to cultivate responsible character and civic friendship. It is a perspective that enhances public life by advancing the capacity to reason in order to make right judgment. In pursuit of such formation those involved acquire habits of civility, prudence, and service. It is unrealistic to presume that people become good persons without an effort of self-cultivation that is backed by institutional involvement.

Stewardship, Management, and Accountability

The most important task at this point of the discussion is to identify methodologies that can transform the dynamics of land management. Let us begin with a set of two questions for brain-storming. Can we form broad-based structures that will guarantee responsible stewardship for common heritage? Can we identify methodologies of management and accountability for promoting efficiency in public institutions? The answer to these questions points to the claim that responsible management of public property cannot be guaranteed without making reference to the formation of citizens in civic virtues.[71] This demand requires market relations to be connected to the effort of linking civic virtue to civic responsibility.

Stewardship refers to the management of common resources while accountability pertains to the responsibility to give an account to the public on how those resources have been used. Stewardship, management, and accountability are founded on the virtues designed to promote the common good. The reason is that a lasting reform requires more than a mere change of leaders considered to be inefficient, for efficiency is a product of a formed character. Civic virtues, often recognized as social capital, entail respecting rights-claims required for democratic governance. The process necessitates reformulation of the inherited traditions of social organization and the common good. It is a dream that could be realized insofar as "we call for a renewal of the common good tradition along the pluralist-analogical lines that can stand for human rights and social justice."[72] Management and accountability require the sense of civic responsibility, which is not simply a claim to pursue private interest, but responsibility to participate in public life as a measure of the communion of persons living together.[73]

The growing trend of selling land rights is a setback to the efforts intended to alleviate poverty. The state is required to establish a bill that can uphold accountability regarding the sale of the common good. It must be clear that these resources are very often used to deepen inequalities as well as stimulate resentment among those who do not benefit from the improper practices. People have a right to hold public officials accountable when they abuse the power that is entrusted to them for the service the public good. A democratic culture requires the governance of public institutions to be accountable to the people who are served by those institutions. Public administration must put an emphasis on building a political culture that is free of manipulation. It is expected to provide a good example in terms of management and governance. This will be possible insofar as people are helped to know how to work together for the common good. Institutions without conscience and immature political culture embedded in the cloud of selfishness make it difficult to establish stable democracies. A single referendum and occasional elections are not enough. Continuous and inclusive participation in the process of decision-making is indispensable.

Public accountability is maintained by cultural traditions operating through public institutions, which comprise moral values. Institutions guide people the way they behave, work, and decide, both in the private and the public spheres. Sometimes those who are entrusted with authority make decisions that favor private interest. Institutions must realign power in such a way that those in authority cannot abuse it. A successful privatization requires institutions that can stand for the common good. This is possible by maintaining a balance between wealth creation and wealth distribution.

The public deserves to receive accountability on the use of common resources, management, and decision-making. Management includes the ability to understand and select appropriate procedures and policies that can enhance effective governance. Those involved must be people who can interpret the changing conditions of life and identify emerging problems in view of addressing them before it is too late. The dynamics of management ought to be orderly so that decision-making procedures are clearly defined, information is allowed to flow without distortion, and authority takes public responsibility into account, although this process must not be rigid to the extent of impeding spontaneity, imagination, and creativity.

In some cases the management of public institutions does not focus on efficiency. Things are done for private gain. Appointments favor friends, relatives, and cronies, those who are bereft of management aptitudes. Institutional planning is organized with a focus on political power instead of economic rationale. Those who are heading public institutions are political appointees, people who are without merit, skill, or concern for the common good. They are people who are not worthy to be entrusted with a responsibility to oversee public property.

Stewardship of the common heritage requires public accountability. For good governance, policymakers are required to present, regularly and with clarity, their intentions, reasons, strategies, and performance standards to the public. Public accountability requires those in positions of authority to take responsibility by explaining how they are implementing the duties that are entrusted to them because they affect everybody. People need explanations from their leaders and stewards whose decisions and actions affect public life. It is interesting to note that those in positions of authority make final decisions without consulting the people concerned. This is how power is exercised. It then becomes too late to stop them when the damage is already done. The rationale for knowing the motive before the action is to limit the potential damage of some decisions that are taken on behalf of the public. Yet, in most cases, governance structures lack well-defined procedures that can prevent those in authority from causing harm. The existing structures lack mechanisms for checks and balances that can enable people to hold authorities accountable.

The population allows authorities to maintain barriers of secrecy around their motivations and decisions so that they no longer feel obliged to explain themselves to the public. Consequently, the authorities are left free to act in the most irresponsible ways. They, in fact, act as if the countries they lead are private properties belonging to them. The situation is worsened by a general lack of performance standards that are agreed upon and against which the authorities can be held accountable. In a similar vein, the lack of such ethical standards allows those in authority to ignore their responsibility to give an account to the public.

Participation of all citizens in the process of decision-making is crucial for good governance. Those who are in positions of authority are so powerful that they can sell land rights to foreign investors and evict indigenous people from their ancestral lands without public consent. It is possible that the policymakers do not fully understand their responsibility, which includes explaining the intended objective, performance, and the means used to undertake the duties that are assigned to them. In most cases, such a mental framework is supported by outdated traditions in which a chief is not questioned, challenged, or held accountable.

People cannot monitor what goes on in their country if they do not know what those in positions of authority are doing. For a democratic system, giving an account to the public is a responsibility that cannot be avoided. People have the right to hold leaders accountable for whatever they are doing for the sake of the public good. Blind loyalty and partisan trust leave those responsible unchallenged to the extent of doing whatever they want. The aim of holding to account those responsible is to get the necessary information the public needs in order to be able to voice their opinion on matters of common interest. Checks and balances are indispensable for good governance and responsible leadership.

Meanwhile, we have not developed an effective procedure for governance that can hold those responsible accountable. The reason is that we have not created management control systems and performance standards that can halt potential damage before it happens. It means that we have allowed those in positions of authority to have more power than the people. Consequently, when leaders wield more power than the public the worst can happen. To avoid such an extreme situation the public must identify performance standards to be expected of their leaders and establish structures, modalities, and procedures for assessment. This is how to stop the widespread plunder of natural resources and abuse of public office. People must be courageous enough to hold public officials accountable for abusing authority entrusted to them to serve the common good. The reform of public institutions goes together with the formation of character as well as the setting up of ethical standards for stewardship, management, and accountability.

The free market, after the fall of communism, has been presented as the only system that can promote economic development.[74] It is true that the market motivates human creativity and efficiency in order to increase production. But it has been observed that the free market is presented as the only solution to the problems underlying economic development without paying attention to the structural weaknesses within itself. This observation reminds us that there is a need to introduce critical analyses to the debate concerning the relationship between land, market, and morality. The growing suspicion over the role of the free market shows that a critical analysis of the relationship between land, market, and morality is required. Effective land management systems depend on the transformation of moral behavior and social conditions of life. This requirement entails challenging all forms of injustice, providing people with effective means of becoming responsible citizens, encouraging participation, guaranteeing freedom of exchange of goods, and building effective institutions.

It is true that market investment is good for economic growth.[75] But efficiency in public institutions is required in order to monitor as well as challenge extremes of the market. The market should be moved by generous passion for wealth creation and the common good instead of private interest at the expense of the majority. There must be a way to examine, publicly, the trend of selling land rights to foreign investors. We have to pay attention to the market approaches that do not respect moral values. It is a risk to take for granted that every person is able to avoid extreme passions, thereby presuming that every person is able to shun selfishness and greed. There are no short-cuts in the task of eradicating poverty. We have to face it by admitting that the free market cannot be an instant remedy to economic problems. We have to strengthen public institutions in order to establish a balance between institutions that regulate the public sphere, enforce ethics of responsibility, and uphold the fact that the market and morality complement each other.[76]

It is evident that the market could be unreliable and destructive, but we cannot promote economic advancement, based on exchange of goods, without the role of the market. The market is a two-edged sword: it can either enhance economic advancement or breed unethical behavior. It is not wise to throw out the baby with the bathwater, or throw out the baby and keep the bath-water. The challenges we have raised in this discourse could be addressed in a concerted effort and shared responsibility. The success of the market is not automatic. Its success is achieved by linking its dynamics to the process of interiorizing civic obligations that are founded on civic virtues, promoting creative participation, and shaping public institutions.

The market, argues Jonathan Sacks, "does not survive by market forces alone."[77] It also depends on other institutions, which are expressions of human experience. It could be said that the market is not only a place for exchange of material goods; rather, it is a place for exchanging the totality of human experiences emanating from different institutions that are intended to maintain a balance in social relations. The free market does not automatically generate economic prosperity; rather, there must be public institutions that can challenge its excesses. If that is the case, then the market must be perceived as a contested sphere where struggles between private interest and public interest take place.

In the early years of independence, Jomo Kenyatta, the first President of the Republic of Kenya, said that "land is the heritage we received from our forefathers. In land lies our salvation and survival."[78] This exhortation exerts pressure on public officials, those who are designated as guardians of the common heritage, to be responsible. The existing problems of land management could be linked to the problems of moral formation, disintegration of moral traditions, socio-political organization, and institutional governance. To address the situation, it is the responsibility of the citizens to establish viable methodologies of reform, formation in civic virtues, and to take initiative in correcting the situation from the grassroots level to the national and international levels.

Notes

[1] The notion of privatization, in this chapter, is explored more deeply than it was presented in the first chapter. The focus here is on the meaning, function, and limitation. This analysis aims at creating awareness in the way we make reference to the ideology of privatization and how it has influenced the land rights debate.

[2] For the insights of this paragraph I am indebted to the overview of Future Agricultures, "Land Grabbing in Africa and the New Politics of Food," *http://www.r4dfid.gov.uk.pdf/outputs/futureagriculture/FAC_Policy_Brief_No401.pdf* (Accessed November 24, 2013).

[3] The project of producing bio-fuel as a renewable and cleaner source of energy to avoid environmental destruction sounds plausible. Its validity is, however, questionable because evicting indigenous people from their ancestral lands to facilitate the project is ethically incorrect. The poor will not benefit the project because this need does not emerge from local context. It is a project destined to furnish the foreign markets.

[4] Jacqueline M. Klopp, "Pilfering the Public: The Problem of Land Grabbing in Contemporary Kenya," *Africa Today* 47, 1 (Winter 2000): 7-26, at 16.

[5] The Ndungu Report, "Land Graft in Kenya," *Review of African Political Economy* 32, 103 (March 2005): 142-151, at 142. This report was prepared by a national commission assigned to investigate and present a report on corruption in land management to the parliament.

[6] Joseph Khamisi, *The Politics of Betrayal: Diary of the Kenyan Legislator* (Trafford: Trafford Publishing, 2011), 5.

[7] The Ndungu Report, "Land Graft in Kenya," 143.

[8] Ibid., 145.

[9] Klopp, "Pilfering the Public: The Problem of Land Grabbing in Contemporary Kenya," 9.

[10] Ibid., 18.

[11] Ambreena Manji, *The Politics of Land Reform in Africa: From Communal Tenure to Free Markets* (London: Zed Books, 2006), 1, 20.

[12] These authors cover a period of three decades, from 1980s to the present.

[13] In the discussion, terms "morality" and "ethics" are used interchangeably.

[14] Amartya Sen, *On Ethics and Economics* (Oxford: Blackwell Publishers, 1987), Preface.

[15] Ibid., 1.

[16] Ibid., 8.

[17] Ibid.

[18] John Milbank, *Theology and Social Theory: Beyond Secular Reason* (Cambridge: Blackwell Publishers, 1993), 237-238.

[19] Sen, *On Ethics and Economics*, 26.

[20] Ibid., 25.

[21] Philip Wogaman, *Economics and Ethics* (Philadelphia: Fortress Press, 1986), 15.

[22] Ibid., 17.

[23] Ibid., 15-16.

[24] This way of thinking is founded upon the argument that a human person is dominated by the pressure to make money as the ultimate purpose of human life. And as such economic prosperity cannot be subordinated to other spheres of human experience. For further elaboration, see Max Weber, *The Protestant Ethic and the Spirit of Capitalism*, translated by Talcott Persons (New York: Dover Publications Inc., 2003), 47-78.

[25] Olivier De Schutter, "How Not to Think of Land-Grabbing: Three Critiques of Large-Scale Investments in Farmland," *Journal of Peasant Studies* 38, 2 (March 2011): 249-279, at 262.

[26] Garric Small and John Sheehan, "Selling Your Family: Why Customary Title is Incomparable to Western Conceptions of

Property   Value,"
http://www.academia.edu/1396111/selling_Your_Family_Why_customary
_title_is_incomparable_to_Western_Conceptions_of_Propety_value
(Accessed October 20, 2013).

    [27] Wogaman, *Economics and Ethics*, xi.

    [28] Ibid., 12.

    [29] Christian A. Conrad, *Morality and Economic Crisis: Enron, Subprime & Co.* (Hamburg: Diplomica Verlag, 2010), 65.

    [30] This analysis is far beyond the competition between socialism versus capitalism. Both of them are extreme forms of development theory because they tend to favor a certain section of the society. And consequently they end-up becoming unrealistic. My concern goes beyond these two economic ideologies that I honorably consider incomplete. There is no room here for such a debate.

    [31] Robert Skidelsky, "The Moral Vulnerability of Markets," *http://www.economistview.typepad.com/economistview/2008/03/morality-and-ma-html* (Accessed November 21, 2013).

    [32] Ibid.

    [33] Michael J. Sandel, *What Money Can't Buy: The Moral Limits of Markets* (New York: Farrah, Straus, and Giroux, 2012), 5-6.

    [34] Ibid., 6.

    [35] Ibid., 7.

    [36] Ibid., 9.

    [37] Ibid., 14.

    [38] Ibid., 28.

    [39] Ibid., 32.

    [40] Ibid., 48.

    [41] Ibid., 96.

    [42] Lawrence Busch, *The Eclipse of Morality: Science, State, and Market* (New York: Walter de Gruyter Inc., 2000), 99.

43 Sandel, *What Money Can't Buy: The Moral Limits of Markets*, 111.

44 Ibid., 119.

45 Ibid., 127.

46 Ali Velshi, "Is It Possible to Have Morality in a Free Market?" *http://www.q2.com/105311/is-it-possible-to-have-morality-in-a-free-market* (Accessed November 19, 2013).

47 Christian A. Conrad, *Morality and Economic Crisis: Enron, Subprime & Co.* (Hamburg: Diplomica Verlag, 2010), 65.

48 Ibid., 65-66.

49 Baron de Montesquieu, *The Spirit of the Laws*, trans. Anne Cohler, Basia Miller, and Harold Stone (Cambridge: Cambridge University Press, 1989), 18. Montesquieu, a French political philosopher who lived during the period of enlightenment, is famous for the articulation of the theory of separating political powers. Checks and balances must be applied as a device to prevent tyranny. His insights have immensely championed ideas of institutional interaction, participatory democracy, social justice, and the common good.

50 For verification, see the official presentation of Savior Mwambwa, "Tax Exemptions, Capital Flight, and Tax Havens: The Role of Multinational Companies," Center for Trade Policy and Development, *http://www.afrodad.org/presentations/savior-mwambwa-presentation-tax-havens.pdf* (Accessed December 24, 2013)

51 Robert A. Sirico, *Defending Free Market: The Moral Case for a Free Economy* (Massachusetts: Regnery Publishing Inc., 2012), 19.

52 Richard M. Coughlin, *Morality, Rationality, and Efficiency: New perspectives on Socio-Economics* (New York: M.E. Sharpe Inc., 1991), 135.

53 Ibid., 136-137.

54 Ibid., 137.

[55] Clarifications are found in the assessment of Hernando De Soto, *The Mystery of Capital: Why Capitalism Triumphs in the West and Fails Everywhere Else* (New York: Basic Books, 2000).

[56] For a comprehensive study on corruption, see the summary of the report compiled by former chief justice of Tanzania, Joseph Warioba, "The Report of the Warioba Commission on Corruption," *Business Times Supplement* (June 27, 1997): 1-33.

[57] John Powelson, *The Moral Economy* (Michigan: University of Michigan Press, 1998), 142.

[58] Cited by Powelson from David Pryce-Jones, "Corruption Rules the World," *The America Spectator* (December 1997): 27.

[59] Powelson, *The Moral Economy*, 143.

[60] Ibid., 144.

[61] Ibid., 159.

[62] The Ndungu Report, "Land Graft in Kenya," 17.

[63] Southern African Catholic Bishops Conference, "A Call to Examine Ourselves in the Widespread Practice of Corruption," *National Catholic Reporter* (October 21, 2013). This letter is also available at *http://ncronline.org* (Accessed November 20, 2013).

[64] Mahmood Mamdani, *Scholars in the Marketplace: The Dilemmas of Neo-Liberal Reform at Makerere* (Kampala: Fountain Publishers, 2007), 105, 262-268.

[65] This perception was instituted during the period of colonization. Studies in ethics were not a part of academic formation, notably in public universities because of the fear that it could instigate students to think radically with a possibility of revolting against the forces of colonization. The dimension of ethics in areas of philosophy, belief systems, and political economy were fairly introduced recently. Some higher learning institutions, to the present day, continue with the old academic organization in which decolonization of curriculum is not acknowledged. A number of public universities do not have departments of

philosophy, religious studies, theology, or ethics. Is it possible to have well-formed scholars in law, human rights, political science, social ethics, and economics without the study of ethics? The lack of formation in ethics is one of the root causes of the practice of corruption in public institutions.

[66] Donald C. Menzel, *Ethics of Management for Public Administrators: Building Organizations of Integrity* (New York: M.E. Sharpe, 2000), 8.

[67] Maulana Wahiddudin, "How to Eradicate Corruption," *http://www.articles.timesofindia.indiatimes.com/2011-09-16/new-age-insight/30160787-1-spiritual-values-corruption-inculcate* (Accessed November 7, 2013).

[68] Conrad, *Morality and Economic Crisis: Enron, Subprime & Co.*, 71.

[69] Ibid.

[70] Ibid., 75.

[71] Virtue, as a moral excellence, is an interior quality situated between being and action that entails self-cultivation. Any initiative geared toward the reform of the public institutions cannot succeed without paying attention to the character formation, which is the primary sphere of virtue. The reform of the public institutions requires transformation of the mind and the heart of the citizens as a starting point.

[72] David Hollenbach, S.J., "The Common Good Revisited," *Theological Studies* 50, 1 (March 1989): 70-94, at 88.

[73] Ibid.

[74] These insights are well elaborated by Michael Edwards, "The Challenges of Civil Society in Africa," *http://www.trustafrica.org* (Accessed October 23, 2013).

[75] A useful analysis underlying this assertion is given by Adebayo Olukoshi, "Property Rights, Investment, Opportunity and Growth: Africa in a Global Context," in Julian Quan et al., eds.,

Land in Africa: Market Asset or Secure Livelihood (London: Royal African Society, 2004), 25-34, at 26.

[76] For further elaboration, see the article of Wayne Baker and Melissa Forbes, "Moral Values and Market Attitudes," *http://www.webuser.bus.umich.edu/wayneb/pdfs/sociology/moral-values-and-maraket-attitudes.pdf* (Accessed December 12, 2013).

[77] Jonathan Sacks, "Markets and Morals," *The First Things* (September 2000) *http://www.firstthings.com/article/2007/01/markets-and-morals-34* (Accessed December 4, 2013).

[78] Jomo Kenyatta, *Suffering Without Bitterness* (Nairobi: East African Publishing House, 1968), 23.

Chapter 3

Migration, Resettlement, and Integration

A memorable point that emerged from the preceding chapter confirmed that the meanings, values, and functions of land are extended to different dimensions of human experience. Such a perspective persuades us to acknowledge that land disputes are also fuelled by human migrations resulting from civil war, environmental degradation, population growth, and eviction. It is true, as Bill Derman argues, that "as the promise of industrialization and job creation fades away, the availability of farmland to secure livelihood will unlikely diminish."[1] The scarcity of land generates conditions that result in the scramble for farmland, freshwater, and pasture.[2] The increasing land disputes confirm the argument that there is a strong connection between scarcity, migration, and conflict.

Studies on migrants, refugees, and internally-displaced persons have largely focused on reporting the plight of the people uprooted from their homes.[3] There has been limited interest focused on the initiatives of resettlement, integration, and reconstruction of their livelihoods and social relations. Most of the existing analyses are limited to the legal framework that does not focus on causes and consequences.[4] It is evident that when the ethical dimension is ignored, critical questions are not asked and areas of great importance remain unexplored.

The purpose of this chapter is to extend the discourse on land rights disputes toward the trends of migration, resettlement, and integration. It focuses on the argument that the availability of farmland moderates decisions of resettlement and integration. The reasons underlying the need for farmland correspond to the assumption that access to farmland provides livelihood, security, and status. In search for a long-term solution to the problems surrounding initiatives of resettlement and integration, the discussion examines the causes and effects of landlessness, the status of migrants and refugees, indigenization of land rights, citizenship without integration, and the ambiguities of belonging and citizenship.

Landlessness, Statelessness, and Deprivation

In the last four decades people have migrated in great numbers from their countries of origin to exile. Most of them have been forced to migrate because of insecurity resulting from civil wars. The situation was followed by the needs of resettlement and integration for migrants, refugees, and internally-displaced persons. Displacement resulted in the loss of farmland, and migrants and refugees were denied the right to access land in the countries that received them.

Landlessness occurs when people are forced to migrate, are evicted, or are displaced. Those who are dependent on land for their livelihood become impoverished because of the lack of formal employment and other income generating activities. Peasants, as people who entirely depend on land for their subsistence, are the main victims of displacement. Landlessness, for migrants and refugees, is often accompanied by statelessness, deprivation, and exclusion.[5] It is true that landlessness adds to the causes of migration, impoverishment, and insecurity, but one cannot say there is a shortage of arable land in Africa. Shortages are caused by environmental destruction and restricted access. Other causes of land shortage include landholding for speculation, unequal distribution, and inaccessibility due to the lack of the means of transport, market, and security.[6]

Landlessness is a condition that alienates people from the foundation upon which their livelihood is based. It is a form of deprivation because those concerned lose both natural and man-made capital. And unless the basis of people's productive systems are reconstructed, as income generating employment, landlessness could become a source of impoverishment.[7]

Historical records show that the condition of landlessness was created by colonization. To support the argument, Radha Sinha writes:

> Foreign intervention undermined the earlier cohesion of village life with its elaborate, though informal, structure of rights and obligations. Landlords were given sufficient freedom and unrestricted rights to dispose of land without any reference to the village community except in some cases where the disposal of wasteland was vested in the village community. The farmlands belonging to the grassroots communities were taken over by European settlers, leaving natives to subsist on poor lands.[8]

Landlessness occurred during the period of colonization. But most of it today is attributed to the failure of the post-colonial governance systems. Many countries, six decades after independence, have not changed the administrative structures inherited from the colonial masters. Consequently, the colonial method is applied by the post-colonial administration when farmlands are forcefully taken from the small-scale farmers. Creation of migrant peasants, squatters, and evictees has added to the number of the landless. Effects of landlessness include unemployment, vulnerability, and impoverishment.[9]

The loss of land has long-term effects for those who depend entirely on agriculture for their livelihood. Even after resettlement it could take many years for them to be organized. The reason is that landlessness is accompanied with the loss of socio-economic status that renders the people concerned vulnerable and impoverished. It takes many years to recover because landlessness is accompanied with the loss of cultural context, survival mechanisms, and social status. It is from such a perspective that resettlement becomes a process of reconstructing livelihoods and social relations.

People become stateless when their nationality ceases to exist for various reasons. It could happen when the land on which they live is taken by another nation, when the country disintegrates, when they become refugees and their land is taken, or claims of ownership cannot be proved due to the lack of formal documentation. Statelessness, in one way or another, is related to the condition of being landless. From an administrative standpoint, African countries are reluctant to correct the injustice of land expropriation as well as promote equitable access to land through redistributive reforms.

Many people, similarly, become stateless as a result of arbitrary denial of the rights of belonging and citizenship. There are many difficulties which stateless people contend with. It includes the denial of opportunities to establish "legal residence, travel, work in the formal economy, send children to school, access basic healthcare services, own property, vote, hold elected office, and enjoy the protection and security of a country."[10] Statelessness, as a denial of membership and citizenship rights to individuals, groups, or communities, generates insecurity, marginalization, and exclusion. The denial of citizenship renders migrants stateless with a possibility of undermining their right to own land. In some countries, apparently, the condition has caused conflict. Cote d'Ivoire and Democratic Republic of Congo are good examples.

There is a longstanding perception that migrants and refugees are unwanted foreigners. The perception arises from the sentiment of resentment and competition for resources. But hostile feelings are more complex than a generalized resentment premised on the economic status.[11] Problems pertaining to landlessness and statelessness, as formal structures of deprivation and exclusion, are far from being resolved because processes of resettlement and integration are not considered as a long-term solution of unemployment for migrants and refugees.

Complex structures of inequality and competing claims intended to access land need an examination that must be conducted in such a way that they benefit everybody regardless of one's origin and culture.[12] Effects of landlessness and statelessness could be properly understood insofar as we engage ourselves in the task of evaluating the scope of the prevailing land disputes. To do that the next section examines the validity of the claims of membership, status, and security from the standpoint of migrants, refugees, and internally-displaced persons.

Membership, Status, and Security

Resettlement is a multifaceted process because it is attached to the claims of membership, status, and security. According to Mahmood Mamdani, traditional communities "are built around their members' adherence to values, norms, and traditions that bear a prescriptive value for their identity, and failure to comply with them affects their own understandings of membership."[13] People's perceptions of migrants as foreigners affect processes of membership, status, and security.

Most of the African people are peasants and herders, and for them it is access to land that guarantees membership, status, and security. It is not that "membership and status automatically entail rights, but they make it legitimate to claim them."[14] Land-based resource is a significant investment for the poor people, and it is widely perceived as a means to secure livelihood and social status. From a legal viewpoint, migrants and refugees are not allowed to enter into land transactions, because in doing so the process confers the status of citizenship which entitles them to the right to own property. Policymakers believe that access to land is accompanied with the process of incorporation into the population. It is from such a perspective that I argue access to land moderates the claims of resettlement, integration, and citizenship.

The set-up of the traditional communities usually tends to promote conditions that can guarantee them security, status, and privilege. The process uses the claims of the first-comer, kinship, and native as attributes of self-assertion. In this process, clearly, status provides a possibility that can guarantee access and control of the resources. Migrants and minorities, depending on certain contexts and circumstances, play the role of underdog by hiding within the political landscape in search of a secure way to survive. They may identify themselves with the dominant groups. But when an opportunity arises they would come out to claim their true identity. Such is a pattern underlying the exercise of rights and "the practice of political agency that can change identities."[15]

During the colonial period the claim of customary entitlement was strengthened by the colonial policy that tied privilege to the native status and territorial integrity.[16] Land ownership created a distinction between natives and migrants because it was a way of raising one's status. In recent years, apparently, the relation between natives and migrants has been affected by the scarcity of farmland and the competition that ensues.

Competition for land, water, and pasture between peasants and herders has been generating tension at the grassroots level. In the case of Tanzania, for example, land-related clashes are common in Morogoro and Arusha regions. For decades, deadly clashes have been raging between peasants and herders in search for farmland, water, and pasture. This situation is also common in northern regions of Kenya, north-east of Uganda, and elsewhere. In order to resolve the situation there must be a formalized plan of land use, reform of land rights systems, and effective management.[17] A genuine solution must focus on formulating long-term policies that require participation of the people concerned. These conflicts prevail because communal ownership systems rarely define the occupied territory and reach of their claims with precision. The homeland, where one can claim native status, could be as narrowly conceived as the land controlled by a clan or a village. Claims of this sort are usually upheld by narratives that cannot be verified empirically.

At the grassroots level, as I have mentioned earlier, land is among the leading causes of conflict, and the concern for the indigenous people is to protect their land. The need arises from the rationale that livelihood and survival of their cultural traditions and belief systems depend on the protection of the land they inherited from their ancestors. A person who owns land is regarded as having a defined socio-economic status in the society. From such a perspective one could say that land ownership provides membership, livelihood, status, and security.

The rising of identity politics, in recent years, is strongly attached to the quest for security and the sense of belonging as a reaction toward "the global trends of deterritorialization and homogenization."[18] The boundary between natives and migrants is drawn along the claims of land ownership. Land ownership becomes a criterion of distinguishing first-comers from the late-comers. Such a perspective maintains class difference, status, and privilege. Inability to overcome the separation has virtually become an impediment toward the effort of building cohesive societies.

For many cultures, indigenous people are identified with a particular territory as homeland, and access to land provides every member of the community a possibility of livelihood, recognition, and status. Such a condition makes migrants struggle to access land as a means of becoming permanent members, while natives struggle to exclude them in order to minimize competition.[19] Natives see migrants as competitors for limited resources and enemies instead of allies in the struggle to improve conditions of life. The right to land ownership makes a distinction between natives and migrants. It guarantees status of membership within the host community. The idea that citizens, regardless of their origin and status, should have access to resources is theoretically acknowledged. But there are no conditions that can guarantee its realization on the ground.

Concerning marginalized status of the migrants I prefer to present, though briefly, two examples, namely, the Banyamulenge people of the Democratic Republic of Congo and the Nubians of Kenya. The Banyamulenge are believed to be of the Banyarwanda origin living in South Kivu region. The population of the Banyamulenge, according to René Lemarchand, is estimated to be about half a million.[20] It could also be said that they form one of the minority groups living between East Africa and Central Africa.

Historically, the Banyamulenge were described as people who came to the eastern part of the Democratic Republic of Congo as migrants in search for labor or as refugees running away from the wars of Rwanda and Burundi. They are people living in the region lying between Burundi, Rwanda, and Democratic Republic of Congo. Their presence, from the perspective of socio-political status, raises crucial questions related to the rights of belonging, ownership, citizenship, and integration. Meanwhile, the status and membership of the Banyamulenge are highly contested. The situation stands out today as a point of contention between the Democratic Republic of Congo and Rwanda.

The vulnerability of the Banyamulenge has been increasing since 1885, the time when the claims of indigenous and non-indigenous emerged. Some communities defined themselves as indigenous as an attempt to distinguish themselves from the migrant communities. Claims of unspecified identity, loyalty, and statelessness have become a status attributed to the people who belong to border communities and migrants. The dominant communities, in search for a way to dominate migrants, claimed that only those who could prove paternity from someone resident in the Democratic Republic of Congo before the declaration of the Berlin Conference in 1885 would qualify for citizenship. In this case, non-Congolese people were identified following the criterion of the Berlin Conference as a point of demarcation. The Banyamulenge, to the present, whose families had come to the Democratic Republic of Congo as laborers, are perceived as unwanted migrants.

The situation shows that the Banyamulenge are people who have been moving from one place to another, and such a condition has become a source of marginalization to their political status. Such a problematic condition arises from the lack of specific territory of attachment. The situation, consequently, renders them stateless because they are unwanted by the three countries.

Turning to the Nubians of Kenya, historical records show that most of them are descendants of the Nubians of Sudan. The following extract from Adam Hussein Adam unveils the reasons that brought them to Kenya:

The vast majority of the Nubians of East Africa are descendants of Sudanese ex-servicemen in the British army. Following a mutiny in 1897 the British rescinded its decision to repatriate them and instead dispersed the community into Kenyan territory. The Nubians, who by then retained no ties with Sudan and had no claim to land in that country, could not return independently to Sudan and were left with no choice but to remain in Kenya. The Kenyan government uses both ethnicity and territory to establish belonging. Since both Nubian ethnicity and their territory of occupancy are contested, most Nubians live as stateless persons without adequate protection under national law. Above all, [they] live in temporary structures throughout Kenya and often on contested lands. Most Nubians' settlements do not have title deeds and are only occupied temporarily.[21]

The Nubians of Kenya are treated as landless and stateless people. People without national identity and social status are deprived of the right to participation, security, and ownership. Even if they are given a national identity card, because of the international pressure, the political landscape still puts them on the margins. Meanwhile, the way of portraying them as unwanted people remains unchanged.

What conclusions can we draw from the experiences of the Banyamulenge and the Nubians? The question whether the Banyamulenge belong to the Democratic Republic of Congo, Rwanda, or Burundi, is irrelevant. The same could be said for the Nubians, whether they belong to Kenya or Sudan. What is required is to address conditions that jeopardize their political status. Morally speaking, there is no alien, illegal, or stateless person, group, or community in the world. The condition of the Banyamulenge and Nubians

113

shows that African countries have to address issues of migration, resettlement, and integration in a constructive way in order to transcend attitudes of resentment, discrimination, and exclusion.

The Banyamulenge and Nubians are citizens of their country of residence. Because of inevitable historical circumstances they are people who belong to the country they find themselves in. It is inappropriate to identify individuals, groups, or communities as stateless. The challenges encountered by these people necessitate further inquiry with a focus on the evolving meanings of belonging and citizenship. There are many examples of this type in Africa today.

The status of being a migrant generates deprivation of the right to own property. For some countries, there is "differentiated and hierarchical citizenship, with both citizenship by naturalization and registration being categorized as inferior to the citizenship by birth to the extent that the former could be revoked at the discretion of administrative officials."[22] For them, apparently, "paternity is the locus for granting citizenship, which is an important ingredient for realizing basic rights. But some categories of persons, notably migrants, minorities, and women will access them with difficulty."[23]

Indigenization of land rights emerge as a way of maintaining status and guaranteeing security for the natives. This structure, observes Mahmood Mamdani, is formed by

a set of rules defined by the customary land as a composite of different homeland, each homeland designated to a single native tribe. Only those officially designated as natives could claim land rights in the tribal homelands. As a result, participation in public affairs was no longer the right of all those who lived on the land; instead, it became the exclusive preserve of natives said to belong to the homeland.[24]

The institutionalized inequality between natives and migrants leads to disharmony, mistrust, and conflict. In this case status is accompanied with a distinction of classes of people specifying social relations. It determines as well as grants privilege to those who are considered to be natives, with a possibility of generating mistrust between natives and migrants.

In some countries, certain ethnic groups take monopoly over land ownership.[25] This arrangement has been the source of inter-communal mistrust and civil strife in Rwanda, Burundi, and Kenya. The situation shows that there is a conflict of interest between natives and migrants. It propagates attitudes of discrimination and inequality vis-à-vis the rights of ownership and participation. It could also be said that the system indigenizes land rights and social relations.

Indigenization of membership, ownership, and status is premised upon kinship. In this case, descent becomes the primary way to obtain citizenship, and it is used to exclude others. One could say that land, identity, and citizenship are paradigms of inclusion and exclusion. The situation becomes complex because ethnic ownership "rarely defines the territorial and social reach of its various claims with precision."[26]

When people are displaced it is difficult for them to return to their land due to the lack of formally recognized documentation. People would like to have title deeds, but formal procedures are complicated, and it may take decades to obtain one. The process is deliberately made complex in order to create a favorable condition for soliciting bribes. It is not a farfetched claim to say that African governance systems have played the role of obstructing development.

Rights of refugees, migrants, and asylum-seekers make ethnicity, citizenship, and national boundaries ambiguous. The reason is that, remarks Seyla Benhabib, "[we] are at a point in political evolution when the unitary model of citizenship, which bundled together residence upon a single territory with a single administration of a people perceived to be a cohesive entity, is coming to an end."[27] From another perspective one could argue that migrations of people, so to speak, enhance transformation of traditions and institutions. As long as migrants are in the society they will necessarily affect the general landscape of the population.

The claim of membership, as a means of incorporation, depends upon the priority given to the public good. Critics argue that unrestricted membership could lead to a condition that threatens public order. Their dissatisfaction is founded upon the argument that the rights of the natives must be protected. If there are restrictions imposed on migrants for public reasons, then priority cannot be given to those seeking membership and incorporation. In many ways, organizational structures have failed to recognize cultural diversity as well as guarantee equal citizenship. And consequently people involved in the situation resort to the use of violence to secure socio-political status within the establishment. Cote d'Ivoire is a good example.

116

A number of societies combine claims of kinship and territory to form principles and norms of belonging, ownership, and citizenship. It is not easy "to find a modern state where one cannot find close kin living in clusters, associating more with each other than with strangers."[28] Kinship ties form traditions, communities, and homelands. Kinfolk staying closer to one another, following blood ties, form an attachment to a certain territory. Those who live far away from home have a strong attachment to their homeland. This kind of attachment has largely influenced the claims of membership, entitlement, and status.

Membership is accompanied by rights and duties. But because of the generalized migrations, private interest is about to take preference over public interest. To avoid the situation critics argue that restrictive membership is required in order to exclude migrants from the right to own property, hold a public office, and have free movement. To demonstrate the argument, Joseph Carens claims that natives "may do what they like with their own property. They may exclude whomever they want from the land they own."[29] For him, the urge to exclude migrants and refugees from the right of ownership is based upon the argument that the community land belongs to the members of the community only, and as such they have a right to keep out whomever they do not want.[30]

The claims of birthplace, belonging, and kinship are usually presented as a means of protecting oneself against the threat of foreigners. The separation of natives from migrants serves as a protective shield intended to guarantee security for the natives. And in search for a privileged status, natives exploit the condition of foreignness to fend off migrants from the right of land ownership.

The difficulty arises when enforcement of the rights-claims becomes limited. Critics would argue that human rights are only imaginary assumptions removed from history. For them, rights-claims are limited because of self-interest and partisan attitude. Human rights, only enforced by the claims of common humanity, are limited. A number of scholars agree with Carens concerning the argument that "each society has a right to restrict membership to those whom it wishes to admit to its territory. And consequently a society may distribute its jointly held property as it wishes."[31] Respect for all human beings, as moral persons, is a moral imperative. But the way of honoring this ideal differs from one society to another.

The search for a long-term solution to landlessness for migrants, refugees, and internally-displaced persons, resettlement and integration becomes necessary. The following section attempts to unveil the prevailing problems pertaining to the process of incorporation as well as to suggest methodologies that can change the situation.

Migration, Resettlement, and Integration

In the last two decades, possibilities of resettlement and integration were not presented as a part of resolving problems accompanying migration. The discourse on migration focused mainly on political responsibility with a widespread tendency to direct all the blame on colonization, which is partially untrue. The challenges that the African continent must address, without delay, include resettlement

118

and integration of migrants, long-term refugees, and internally-displaced persons.

For policymakers, migrants and refugees are considered to be temporary people expected to return to their countries. But internally-displaced persons within the country must be permanently resettled.[32] Resettlement is intended to provide a means of livelihood and integration. With such expectation refugees are usually assembled in temporary camps where they survive on food rations and limited income generating activities. But for some of them a return to their countries is a challenge because some wars lasted for many years. The case of the Sudan war, which lasted for about thirty years, is a good example. For others, the idea of returning home is not feasible because they have adapted themselves to the culture of the host countries, and there is no guarantee of regaining the land left behind. Most of the migrants and refugees come from rural areas, and for them farmland is the most valuable asset. Land is the foundation of their economic life, cultural identity, and belief system. For them, access to a cultivatable piece of land to reconstruct their livelihood is crucial.

The reasons for migration are not simply personal, imaginary, or idiosyncratic.[33] Causes of migration could be summed up in five categories. First, the main cause of migration is civil wars. The second category involves the scramble for farmland, freshwater, and pasture in semi-arid areas. The third category is characterized by the growth of population, environmental degradation, discrimination based on ethnic affiliation, natural disaster, and religious belief. The fourth category is constituted by peasants seeking to increase food production as a way of improving their income. The fifth category concerns governments demarcating public land reserves, which identifies areas worthy of conservation and development projects.[34] Some migrants cross national borders to become refugees, while others remain in the country to become internally-displaced persons.

Large-scale movements of migrants and refugees across national borders have occurred in Sudan, Mozambique, Angola, Rwanda, Burundi, Liberia, Sierra Leone, Somalia, Ethiopia, Central African Republic, and Democratic Republic of Congo. Internal displacement has been repeatedly experienced in Kenya, Uganda, and Cote d'Ivoire. Intra-state migrations are often connected to the availability of farmland. This is evident because the African population is mostly constituted by peasants and herders. These reasons support the argument that competition over land is intensifying because of the growing population and movement of people looking for arable land. The common forms of human migration known to Africa are forced migrations and internal displacement. These two trends cause influx of refugees, while internal displacement is caused by development projects, land-grabbing, and eviction. For a number of countries, because of the recurring civil wars, resettling migrants, refugees, and internally-displaced persons is difficult.

The phenomenon of migration is a balancing process of wealth redistribution. Since forced migrations, whether as streams of refugees or not, are not in the interest of migrants and refugees only, they attempt to balance unequal distribution of resources and political power. Incorporation of migrants into the population is an interactive process that transforms both the receiving and the migrant culture. But the "fear of cultural change emphasizes loss rather than

120

increase of options. Migration and incorporation are complex and contested social phenomena."[35]

Migration policies from the perspective of receiving societies, especially those with restrictive conditions, observes Veit Bader, are dominated by short-term strategies, because they do not cover the whole range of possible interventions, and encounter enormous implementation difficulties arising from the requirements of genuine incorporation.[36] The argument of Bader contends that strategic policies encounter unexpected obstacles. The unforeseeable difficulties arise from the evolving conditions which seem to surpass the control of the restrictive policies available. For example, repatriation is interpreted as a war between natives and migrants. This tendency advocates a way of seeing migrants as enemies. The resulting consequences include obstruction of creative ideas of integration.[37]

Resettlement is a process by which migrants and refugees who have fled conflict and other causes of human suffering start a new settlement in another society. But methodologies of resettlement and integration limited to kinship, birthplace, and cultural affiliation contradict the provision of human rights. It is evident that institutions handling human migration require radical reform. This initiative could reduce the number of conflicts because it promotes integration. For example, civil wars that have emerged due to the lack of proper procedure of resettlement and integration are found in the eastern part of the Democratic Republic of Congo, South Sudan, and Cote d'Ivoire.

It is evident that the process of resettlement revolves around the right of land ownership due to the lack of other forms of employment. But resettlement and establishment of

121

livelihoods for migrants are forgotten.[38] The need for justice-oriented modalities of land distribution, unified land rights systems, supervised land use, and integration remain sidelined. Continuous eruption of civil wars makes the situation unfavorable for long-term initiatives of resettlement and integration. The lack of public order makes the situation precarious and unreliable. Resettlement and integration are not issues that could be relegated to the sidelines of development strategies.

Many countries believe that they have no obligation toward migrants and refugees. For them, these groups do not legally form a part of the political community. On this matter I wish to confirm that this argument is flawed because the task of liberating migrants and refugees from the suffering imposed upon them is a moral obligation. Resentment arises simply because they are perceived as competitors for natural resources, employment market, and public services. But in reality this is not the case because they contribute to the economy through their work as casual laborers and taxpayers. The presence of migrants results in socio-cultural interaction and institutional transformation. The struggle to adapt for the sake of survival leads to the change in behavioral patterns. What they seek to maintain is not "the culture of origin but an immediate culture, a lived multifaceted ethnic culture which is heterogeneous and varies according to class, social status, and gender."[39] Cultural diversity generates unexpected social reality.

Some parts of the continent, especially at the grassroots level, have experienced hostilities between migrants and natives instigated by the fight over farmland. This phenomenon is influenced by attitudes of discrimination, intolerance, and eviction. To other countries, especially those emerging from civil war, reallocation of land for the refugees returning from exile has been difficult due to the lack of official documentation. Countries that have experienced this situation include Burundi, Rwanda, and South Sudan.[40]

The rights of migrants are restricted. A political community is essentially sovereign, and as such some communities may choose to be generous in admitting migrants, while others could argue that they are under no obligation to do so.[41] Even if they admit them they are under no obligation whatsoever to make them citizens. Possibilities of granting rights of citizenship and integration to migrants depend on the generosity of the host countries. To some countries, citizenship is an inherited status limited to the criteria of birthplace, kinship, and culture. It cannot be extended to foreigners.

One of the most commonly held assumption concerning refugees is that they are temporary residents. With this assumption they are welcomed as guests. This way of thinking is sometimes questionable because some migrants were born from parents categorized as long-term refugees. Migrations, so to speak, are not always detrimental to the political culture, collective identity, or unity of the establishment. Instead, they introduce a dimension of transformation into the commonwealth. These are processes through which migrants become hermeneutical partners with natives by reinterpreting cultural traditions.[42] Boldly stated, migrations bring a transformative aspect to the local culture. The movement of change generates new forms of relating, institutions, and traditions. The evolution of disaggregated social relations is creating a condition of transcending geographical borders, claims of the majority, and ethnic discrimination. The transformation of the meanings of the political community, through which rights are extended to the migrants by virtue of residence instead of kinship, are "indicators that natives and migrants are not mutually exclusive."[43]

A survey conducted by Michael Cernea, a senior adviser to the World Bank on issues of internally-displaced persons, resettlement, and rural development, shows that a land-based methodology of resettlement and integration appears to be the most effective. According to him,

> Settling displaced people back on cultivatable land as an income generating employment is the heart of the matter in reconstructing livelihoods. Agricultural land-based resettlement schemes have been frequently employed in Africa for creating a new productive basis both for [internally-displaced persons] and refugees. Throughout Africa empirical evidence confirms that replacing land with land, that is, land-based resettlement, is by far a more successful strategy than compensation in cash, which often fails to lead to income restoration, let alone betterment.[44]

Without farmland, as an alternative, the condition of impoverishment would persist. Land-based alternative has proved to be a good recovery form of resettlement and integration.[45] The reason is that industries that can provide employment, as I have mentioned earlier, do not exist. The idea that reconstruction of the livelihoods of African migrants, refugees, and internally-displaced persons is guaranteed by granting farmland is appropriate, realistic, and viable.

The existing systems of national organization have failed to formulate effective methodologies of naturalization for migrants and refugees.[46] The scenario generates a condition whereby natives perceive migrants as enemies. A form of resettlement that is limited to the criteria of birthplace and kinship contradicts provisions of human rights. The existing situation shows that institutions handling human migration need rethinking. Such initiative could reduce the number of conflicts because it promotes integration. Civil wars that have emerged due to the lack of integration are found in the Democratic Republic of Congo and Cote d'Ivoire. Programs of resettlement and integration are successful when they are presented as constitutive strategies of development.

The emergence of identity politics could be interpreted as an expression of the quest for security and self-preservation against "global trends of deterritorialization and homogenization."[47] The boundary between natives and migrants is drawn when avenues of mutual exchange are closed. The pattern becomes a criterion to distinguish first-comers from late-comers. The issue at stake here is that governance systems are characterized by the lack of clear procedure of integration. It is a situation that reflects inability to deal with multiethnic condition to form cohesive societies.

Integration refers to the process of bringing together different social groups. It is founded upon the ideals of social inclusion and social cohesion. It is a process of building social relations in a way that promotes societies which are stable and just. This ideal is based on four moral principles, namely, tolerance, inclusion, solidarity, and participation.[48]

Integration, as a process of appropriation, refers to the "institutional habits that bring individuals together to form a functioning political community."[49] It presupposes a plurality of coexisting worldviews governed by a framework of inclusion. There are four conditions that obstruct integration: first, difficulties of complete integration emerge when there is no historical community to identify with; second, when the nation-state does not provide a clear guideline; third, when natives perceive migrants and refugees as enemies; and fourth, when farmland becomes unavailable.

Integration is not one-way traffic that requires migrants to conform in order to fit into the lifestyle of the host country. Rather, it is two-way traffic that brings together migrants and natives to facilitate mutual accommodation. Such a perspective provides a ground to argue that the process of resettlement and integration do not have a fixed formula. It all depends upon a number of variables, namely, assistance from the receiving society, employment possibilities, and availability of farmland. Successful resettlement and integration require long-term strategies inculcated into the development plan, political determination, and cultural traditions.

Some governments make decisions that affect resettlement when they perceive migrants and refugees as victims of war, and there is no need to integrate them into the general population. For them, access to land is an assurance of permanent integration into the population.[50] But in most cases formalization of the programs of resettlement is not done, and subsequently indigenous people end-up perceiving them as aliens, unwanted, or enemies. Under these conditions they become excluded from participation, ownership, and services. If land and citizenship are not granted, then resettlement and integration, as we have seen in the cases of the Banyamulenge and the Nubians, will be accompanied with conditions of marginalization, exclusion, and impoverishment.

Granting land is an appropriate method for integrating migrants into the population, assuming that they know how to cultivate land. Access to land is important because displacement from homeland takes away the means of production, and land-based resettlement enables them to sustain themselves.[51] Processes of resettlement and integration, nonetheless, need a transition period to rebuild self-confidence. Rebuilding social relations cannot be achieved insofar as migrants are treated as people without rights.

The provision of the United Nations for migrants, refugees, and internally-displaced persons guarantees access to resources, but the reality on the ground is different because there is a strong resentment of resettlement and integration.[52] The situation has been revealed through the expression of xenophobia that has been witnessed in some countries including South Africa. Restrictive migrant policies, accompanied with a shift from human rights to security policies, make it difficult for the integration of the migrants to take place because it cherishes sentiments of intolerance, resentment, and exclusion. The exclusion of the uprooted people raises serious questions. Access to land, naturalization, and integration are among the most contested issues, and the change of the situation is not going to happen overnight. The challenge could be addressed insofar as the project of resettlement and integration is incorporated into development strategies.

The shift from a homogenizing impulse to the management of difference is necessary for transition from a culturally-centered viewpoint of socio-political organization to the plurality of cultural worldviews.[53] It is evident that cultural differences will not disappear overnight because they are more fundamental than political ideologies. Once a society has a large number of people who are not integrated in the general landscape of the population the situation could be a source of civil unrest. The problem is caused by the lack of the idea of permanency on the part of policymakers of the host countries.

Access to land is traditionally connected to the rights-claims of being native, belonging, and citizenship. This approach is, however, considered to be problematic today. The following section examines ambiguities of belonging and citizenship so as to capture the problem of land ownership from the perspective of cultural traditions.

Ambiguities of Belonging and Citizenship

The political tradition of identifying a person with birthplace as a fixed and unchanging variable goes together with the ideologies of uniformity, homeland, and centralization of authority. The perception generates misunderstanding because it tends to ignore rights of migrants. In a similar way, ownership is attached to blood relations. The claims of kinship and birthplace validate one's rights-claims. The idea that each community has its own homeland, that is, each community rightfully belongs to its homeland, or it is native to its homeland, is a widely accepted narrative. People's imaginations confirm that natives must be identified with their homelands.[54] This understanding is the basis for the claim that natives must be attached to their homelands and that the world outside the homelands belongs to other people.

But the claims of indigenous and homeland are increasingly becoming ambiguous and problematic. A number of conflicts, to some countries, are fights over who is indigenous and who is not. The situation has become the source of discrimination, marginalization, and exclusion. It is clear that the situation is associated with inability to create unified systems of social organization. The existing governance systems identify people following the criteria of ancestry and birthplace. The point of concern is how to create a unified framework of belonging and citizenship based on exclusive paradigms. A widespread understanding is that only those who are indigenous can present claims of ownership rights. The system has a negative effect for those who are considered to be migrants.

Narratives of birthplace and belonging are determinant factors in land distribution, ownership, citizenship, and integration. On this account, remarks Mahmood Mamdani,

> When it comes to land there are two claims. One says that land belongs to the native tribe; it is part of the tribal homeland. The other says the land belongs to the nation, the community of citizens; from this point of view, the homeland is a nation-state. The tribal claim is rooted in the imagination of exclusion, and the national claim in the nationalist post-colonial imagination.[55]

129

It is difficult to balance rights-claims with the rationale of belonging.[56] The task of building common citizenship goes together with the challenge of reconciling rights-claims with exclusive cultural traditions.

The claim of belonging is often connected, directly or indirectly, to the land question. But the definition of citizenship is either based on territory, kinship, or residence. These variables converge when the claim of native becomes a means to something else. It is not easy to answer the question of who are natives and who are not. It is not sufficient to say natives are the first-comers. From the viewpoint of the migrants, one could argue that citizenship based on blood relations cannot be the only genuine criterion because the formation of a political community is a continuous process of mutual accommodation founded upon different variables.

Homeland is expressed as a birthplace that accounts for one's identity, originality, and entitlement. It is a right that cannot be denied to individuals, groups, or communities. There are various ways of belonging insofar as there are different types and spheres of belonging. This is a situation that allows an individual to be a citizen without a guarantee of full integration. For example, one could be a citizen but cannot hold a public office. This form of citizenship operates under the paradigm of inclusion and exclusion.

Belonging is ambiguous because it attaches itself to different dimensions of self-realization. Its content changes depending on the context and circumstance. The question attached to belonging and citizenship is who belongs where, and who is entitled to what, and from which dimension of belonging, because there are different categories of belonging. The claim of belonging is increasingly becoming ambiguous because an individual could belong to different countries simultaneously by virtue of birth and residence. Multiple citizenships generate a complex situation because they do not necessarily fall under the criteria of territorial integrity, cultural uniformity, or blood relation.

The claims of birthplace, belonging, and ownership, altogether, must take into account the rights of migrants who form a part of what Seyla Benhabib calls "the rights of others." The fulfilment of the mandate requires political imaginations that can transcend the claims of kinship and birthplace as a basis of common citizenship. There must be a shift from exclusion to inclusion with a possibility of broadening the definition of political community.

From a political viewpoint, a nation-state is expected to bring together all the people living in its territory. The underlying assumption is that there is cohesion that forms the basis of living together despite differing worldviews from one group to another. A democratic state needs participation of all its members in order to make them experience the value of belonging.[57] Realization of such a provision is, nonetheless, facing many difficulties. Among the obvious ones are as follows: first, some nation-states have some communities on its territory belonging to other nation-states; second, citizenship is determined by discriminative criteria based on culture, territory, and kinship; third, multiple identities of belonging and citizenship undermine ideas of cultural uniformity and territorial integrity as a necessary accompaniment to political membership;[58] fourth, people may have formal membership of a nation-state and yet lack specific allegiance.

Can we establish a citizenship that does not depend on belonging to a community based on kinship and birthplace? Citizenship is generally defined as a "membership in a political community based on defined rights and duties."[59] Weaknesses of a number of nation-states include inability to accommodate cultural diversity and the lack of an agreed-upon framework of the common good. Citizenship deals with the challenge of ordering individuals, groups, communities, and institutions. It offers several benefits such as the rights to representation, access to labor markets, security, property ownership, freedom to travel, and social integration. Citizenship, as a matrix of rights and duties governing members of a political community, exists in tension with multiple identities operating at different levels. It is a condition arising from a shared status that has implications for the politics of identity because it claims priority over other identities. Identity politics makes the meanings of belonging and citizenship problematic.

The framework of citizenship, for many years, applied the criteria of kinship and birthplace as primary conditions to confer the right of ownership. Reliance on the interpretation of history as a determinant variable of belonging remains problematic toward the phenomenon of social integration. It is increasingly becoming clear that the claim of native is identified with attitudes of discrimination, marginalization, and exclusion.

Those who advocate exclusive rights claim that access to land must be based on kinship with reference to those who are indigenous to the community. The other category of people inhabiting the land, which include migrants and refugees, is excluded from the right of ownership.

The meanings of belonging and citizenship are always changing. It is true that communities and states

> are built around their members' adherence to values, norms, and traditions that bear a prescriptive value for their identity, in that failure to comply with them affects their own understandings of membership and belonging. Surely, though, there is always contestation and innovation around such cultural definitions and narratives.[60]

This means cultural traditions are always in dialogue with the changing conditions of life. This characteristic alters specific meanings of belonging and citizenship. Such a characteristic indicates that the meanings of belonging and citizenship are always in the process of shifting and transformation.

These variations arise insofar as there are different dimensions and spheres of experience and belonging. Belonging to a nation-state does not mean that all communities within it have the same ancestry, culture, religion, or language. Nation-states, in many ways, have failed to form a basis for cross-cultural communication and mutual accommodation as a means of building a common ground for common citizenship.

The argument of birthplace is used to justify the claims of identity, belonging, and community. The feeling of belonging is built around a specific cultural community. Birthplace is widely used as a way of identifying people because it refers to specific culture and territory. But the framework of the nation-state has not learned how to cope with the changing

133

patterns of migration, diversity, minority, and integration. A number of countries find it difficult to go beyond the traditional thinking of defining political community as an imaginary cultural community and political belonging that entail uniformity.

The claim of belonging plays a role of shaping the claims of entitlement and citizenship. It is at the same time inclusive and exclusive. It is inclusive in the sense that it propagates community. But it can also be exclusive when it overrides the rights of migrants as a means of self-preservation in search for autonomy, security, and self-determination. Belonging and citizenship are at the same time paradigms of inclusion and exclusion. They designate who is indigenous and who is not, which, by extension, guarantees social status and land entitlement.

People belong to different families, groups, and communities, and there are different categories of citizenship, namely, citizenship by virtue of residence and citizenship by virtue of birth. These categories justify formal exclusion of migrants. "Exclusion presents new challenges for the politics of inclusion."[61] Many societies have inherited cultural traditions that exclude women, minorities, and migrants from the right of ownership.[62] They limit themselves to the criteria of birthplace and belonging without any consideration of the rights of others.[63] People need inclusive principles that can govern fairly the life of different communities found in the political establishment. Systems of governance that render people alien in their own country should be categorized as unjust. Identifying people with fixed cultural traditions and territories, in the era of globalization, could increase the number of conflicts.

Another condition worthy of note is citizenship without integration. Granting citizenship may not necessarily alter tendencies of discrimination and exclusion toward those who are considered to be migrants.[64] The situation occurs when migrants are presented as unwanted people for the purposes of socio-political entitlements, including formal employment, education grants, leadership positions, and property ownership. A point worth noting here is that a person is accepted as a citizen by virtue of having formal identification, but the same person is excluded from the right to ownership.

The understanding of citizenship as membership in a political community constituted by fixed cultural traditions, belief systems, and territory reflects a self-enclosed moral system. One could argue that the rights of migrants necessitate transformation of the meanings of belonging and citizenship. Such a perspective entails the need to adjust formal definitions underlying these variables. The process requires us to reconfigure the claim of homeland by redefining its implications of membership, belonging, and entitlement. The crisis of citizenship, argues Mahmood Mamdani, "is not about scarce resources thought to be connected to it. It is about defining access to resources. Citizenship does not entitle you to resources, but it entitles you to enter the struggle around resources."[65]

Belonging and citizenship are ambiguous because they are always changing depending on the prevailing social conditions. Human beings have multiple identities that could be shifted as well as mobilized depending on the prevailing circumstances. The meanings of these concepts are not based on a single variable as a determinant factor. The claims of homeland, belonging, and culture, as basic referents for

135

belonging, membership, and citizenship, are increasingly becoming inadequate to justify citizenship because other criteria such as residence, resettlement, and change of nationality must also be considered.

These ambiguities could be summed up in seven ways. First, to certain cultures, control of resources is restricted to male householders belonging to certain clans; second, formal exclusion applies to migrants and minorities; third, nation-states can only be consolidated internally by applying hostility toward migrants; fourth, citizenship is justified by criteria of kinship, uniformity, and territory; fifth, the model of nation-state founded upon exclusive membership is eroded by cultural diversity; sixth, borderless citizenship is a threat because it overrides requirements of cultural uniformity and kinship; and seven, the claims of belonging and citizenship are "ambiguous because they imply not only inclusion, but also exclusion."[66]

The point of contention here is that the framework of political community is lacking a clear definition because it cannot be restricted to cultural membership and land ownership. We have to create a concept that can transcend the claims of kinship, territory, ownership, and uniformity. According to Joseph Carens,

> One cannot justify restrictions on the grounds that those born in a given territory or born of parents who were more entitled to the benefits of citizenship than those born elsewhere or born of alien parents. Birthplace and parentage are natural contingencies that are arbitrary from a moral viewpoint. One of the primary goals of the common humanity, as a common ground, is to minimize

the effects of such contingencies upon the distribution of social benefits.[67]

Granting citizenship following the criteria of birthplace and ancestry stand in contrast to the moral principles of common humanity, and the requirement of equal treatment ensued. Similarly, citizenship based on culture could be categorized as discriminatory for supporting unjustifiable privilege. Others would argue that exclusion is justified by the right of communities to self-determination, and that migration negatively affects economic well-being as well as the native culture.

The increasing mobility of people raises new questions. The question that arises immediately is: can we constitute the meaning of citizenship without considering the import of cultural identity? The concept of citizenship could be refashioned by challenging the rigid understanding of identity, belonging, and birthplace. In order to guarantee participation for all, the meaning of citizenship should not be limited to one dimension of human experience. Integration of people of diverse cultures requires broadening of the meaning of participation in order to be inclusive.

It is unrealistic to perceive cultural identities as fixed and unchanging realities. Instead, they must be understood as realities of history, which are always affected by the changing conditions of life. In the process of appropriation there is always a transformation. Identities change over time depending on circumstances of life. That is to say claims of belonging and citizenship are immersed in the process of appropriation and reorganization.

While acknowledging that respect for cultural diversity strengthens collective rights, it is also prudent to admit that cultural traditions are limited, and as such they need regular evaluation, self-criticism, and self-transformation. Weaknesses of a citizenship premised on birthplace and cultural uniformity include rigidity, self-centeredness, and exclusion. It presents traditions as unchangeable realities. One could argue that citizenship, as a social construct, should not be approached as an end-in-itself; rather, it must be perceived as a process that is open to change. Following these arguments one could conclude that the meanings of belonging and citizenship are not static because they are always subjected to contestation from within and from without.

The requirement to revisit the claims of birthplace, belonging, and citizenship is not merely a relic of the past. It is a required art to organize modern societies. The prevailing challenge of exclusion raises serious questions with the main concern revolving around the demands of rights and duties. Issues related to the exclusion of the migrants cannot be taken for granted in the process of building a democratic culture, because the problems related to belonging and citizenship are often linked to the rights of the migrants, refugees, and minorities.

Different forms of belonging and citizenship are incomplete, and as such they leave room for contestation and innovation. Causes of the situation derive from the migration of peoples and the changing conditions of life. We need a revised understanding of the claims of belonging and citizenship that can accommodate cultural diversity as well as consider the rights of all. A basic requirement for success is a shared civic culture of tolerance, trust, and participation.[68] The meanings of belonging and citizenship are always changing because of unending migrations of human beings.

Citizenship and land distribution are crucial issues for countries that have experienced intra-state conflicts. The task of establishing common citizenship demands political imagination that can deemphasize exclusion, and instead advocate residence as a basis of common citizenship. The need to reform citizenship policies is the foundation for nation-building, cohesion, and integration, while discrimination and exclusion sow seeds of political unrest, injustice, conflict, and disintegration. The alternative strategy is to develop principles of compromise founded upon the framework of the common good. Such environment of political imagination requires adjustments that can reconcile rights-claims with social justice.

To conclude the discussion one could say that access to land is always attached to the claims of membership, entitlement, and status. But the most important insight that emerged from the discussion shows that there is a need to reconsider the rights of migrants and refugees, especially the rights of resettlement, ownership, and integration. This demand requires us to revisit the claims of birthplace, belonging, and citizenship because they affect the entire landscape of the land rights debate.

Notes

[1] Bill Derman et al., "Introduction," in Bill Derman et al., *Conflicts Over Land and Water in Africa* (Oxford: James Currey Limited, 2007), 1-30, at 1,

[2] Ibid., 5.

[3] See, for example, articles presented in Dietmar Mieth and Lisa Cahill, eds., *Migrants and Refugees* 4 (March 1994); David Hollenbach, S.J., ed., *Driven from Home: Protecting the Rights of Forced Migrants* (Washington, D.C.: Georgetown University Press, 2010).

[4] See Brad K. Blitz and Maureen Lynch, "Statelessness and Deprivation of Nationality," in Brad K. Blitz and Maureen Lynch, eds., *Statelessness and Citizenship: A Comparative Study on the Benefits of Nationality* (Northampton: Edward Elgar Publishing Limited, 2011), 1-22, at 4.

[5] Ranjit Nayak, "Risks Associated with Landlessness: An Exploration Towards Socially-Friendly Displacement and Resettlement," in Michael Cernea and Christopher McDowell, eds., *Risks and Reconstruction: Experiences of Resettlers and Refugees* (Washington, D.C.: World Bank, 2000), 79-126, at 80.

[6] Concerning difficulties surrounding peasantry, especially inaccessibility and market, see articles compiled by Isaria N. Kimambo et al., eds., *Contemporary Perspectives on African Moral Economy* (Dar es Salaam: Dar es Salaam University Press, 2008).

[7] This subject is well-elaborated in the article of Michael Cernea, "Risks, Safeguards, and Reconstruction: A Model for Population Displacement and Resettlement," Michael Cernea and Christopher McDowell, eds., *Risks and Reconstruction: Experiences of Resettlers and Refugees* (Washington, D.C.: World Bank, 2000), 11-55, at 3.

[8] Radha Sinha, *Landlessness: A Growing Problem* (Rome: Food and Agriculture Organization of the United Nations, 194), 25

[9] Bronwen Manby, *Struggles for Citizenship in Africa* (London: Zed Books, 2009), 141.

[10] Brad K. Blitz and Maureen Lynch, "Statelessness and Deprivation of Nationality," in Brad K. Blitz and Maureen Lynch, eds., *Statelessness and Citizenship: A Comparative Study on the Benefits of Nationality* (Northampton: Edward Elgar Publishing Limited, 2011), 1-22, at 2.

[11] Manby, *Struggles for Citizenship in Africa*, 150.

[12] Ibid., 159.

[13] Seyla Benhabib, *The Rights of Others: Aliens, Residents, and Citizens* (Cambridge: Cambridge University Press, 2004), 120.

[14] Christian Lund, *Land Rights and Citizenship in Africa* (Uppsala: Nordiska Afrikainstitutet, 2011), 11

[15] Benhabib, *The Rights of Others: Aliens, Residents, and Citizens*, 169.

[16] Richard Kuba and Carola Lentz, *Land and the Politics of Belonging in Africa* (Boston: Brill and Leiden, 2006), 18.

[17] For further elaboration, see the rationale of formalizing land rights summed up in the analysis of Benjamin T.A. and Christian Lund, "Formalization of Land and Water Rights in Africa," *European Journal of Development Research* 14, 2 (June 2002): 1-10.

[18] Kuba and Lentz, *Land and the Politics of Belonging in Africa*, 14.

[19] Ibid., 2.

[20] See the study of René Lemarchand, *The Dynamics of Violence in Central Africa* (Philadelphia: Pennsylvania University Press, 2009), 10.

[21] Adam Hussein Adam, "Kenyan Nubians: Standing Up to Statelessness," *http://www.fmreview.org/fmrpdfs/fmr32/19-20.pdf* (Accessed February 7, 2014).

[22] Abraham Korir Sing'Oei, "Citizenship in Kenya: The Nubian Case," in Brad K. Blitz and Maureen Lynch, eds., *Statelessness and Citizenship* (Northampton: Edward Elgar Publishing Limited, 2011), 45-65, at 49.

[23] Ibid., 50.

[24] Mahmood Mamdani, *Define and Rule: Native as Political Reality* (Cambridge: Harvard University Press, 2012), 3.

[25] Ibid., 52.

[26] Kuba and Lentz, *Land and the Politics of Belonging in West Africa*, 13.

[27] Benhabib, *The Rights of Others: Aliens, Residents, and Citizens*, 178.

[28] Parker Shipton, *Mortgaging the Ancestors: Ideologies of Attachment in Africa* (New Haven: Yale University Press, 2009), 85.

[29] Joseph H. Carens, "Aliens and Citizens: The Case for Open Borders," in Thomas Pogee and Darrel Mollendorf, eds., *Global Justice: Seminal Essays* (Minnesota: Paragon House, 2008), 211-233, at 214.

[30] Ibid., 216.

[31] Ibid., 217.

[32] Eftihia Voutira and Barbara Hurrel-Bond, "Successful Refugee Settlement: Are Past Experiences Relevant?" in Michael Cernea and Christopher McDowell, eds., *Risks and Reconstruction: Experiences of Resettlers and Refugees* (Washington, D.C.: World Bank, 2000), 56-78, at 59.

[33] Benhabib, *The Rights of Others*, 137.

[34] Various causes of migration are discussed in detail by P. Peters, "Inequality and Social Conflict Over Land in Africa," *Journal of Agrarian Change* 4, 3 (January 2004): 269-314.

[35] Dirk Hoerder, "Fragmented Macrosystems, Networking Individuals, Cultural Change: Balancing Processes and Interactive Change in Migration," in Veit Bader, et al., *Citizenship and Exclusion* (Hampshire: Macmillan Press, 1997), 81-95, at 82.

[36] See, especially, Veit Bader, "The Arts of Forecasting and Policymaking," in Abdoulaye Kane and Todd H. Leedy, eds., *African Migrations: Patterns and Perspectives* (Indiana: Indiana University Press, 2013), 155-174.

[37] Isaie Dougnon, "Migration as Coping with Risk and State Barriers," in Abdoulaye Kane and Todd H. Leedy, eds., *African Migrations: Patterns and Perspectives* (Indiana: Indiana University Press, 2013), 35-58.

[38] Michael Cernea and Christopher McDowell, "Reconstructing Resettlers' and Refugees' Livelihoods," in Michael Cernea and Christopher McDowell, eds., *Risks and Reconstruction: Experiences of Resettlers and Refugees* (Washington, D.C.: World Bank, 2000), 1-10.

[39] Veit Bader, "Introduction," in Veit Bader et al., *Citizenship and Exclusion* (Hampshire: Macmillan Press, 19997), 1-11.

[40] See the survey undertaken by Chris Huggins et al., *Land, Conflict, and Livelihoods in the Great Lakes Region: Testing Policies to the Limit* (Nairobi: African Centre for Technology Studies, 2004).

[41] Carens, "Aliens and Citizens: The Case for Open Borders," 218.

[42] Benhabib, *The Rights of Others: Aliens, Residents, and Citizens*, 169.

[43] Ibid., 176-177.

143

[44] For further elaboration, see Michael Cernea, "Riska, Safeguards, and Reconstruction: A Model for Population Displacement and Resettlement," in Michael Cernea and Christopher McDowell, *Risks and Reconstruction: Experiences of Resettlers and Refugees* (Washington, D.C: World Bank, 2000), 11-55, at 35-36.

[45] Ibid., 37.

[46] Manby, *Struggles for Citizenship in Africa*, 81.

[47] Kuba and Lentz, *Land and the Politics of Belonging in Africa*, 14.

[48] Jeannotte M. Sharon, "Promoting Social Integration: A Brief Examination of Concepts and Issues," *http://www.socialsciences.uottawa.ca/governmence/eng/documents/promoting-social-integration.pdf* (Accessed January 23, 2014).

[49] Seyla Benhabib, *The Rights of Others: Aliens, Residents, and Citizens* (Cambridge: Cambridge University Press, 2004), 121.

[50] Veronique Lassailly-Jacob, "Reconstructing Livelihoods through Land Schemes: Comparative Reflections on Refugees and Oustees in Africa," in Michael Cernea and Christopher McDowell, eds., *Risks and Reconstruction: Experiences of Resettlers and Refugees* (Washington, D.C.: World Bank, 2000), 108-126, at 119.

[51] Eftihia Voutira and Barabara Hurrel-Bond, "Successful Refugee Settlement: Are Past Experiences Relevant?" in Michael Cernea and Christopher, eds., *Risks and Reconstruction: Experiences of Resettlers and Refugees* (Washington, D.C.: World Bank, 2000), 56-78, at 77.

[52] Kuba and Lentz, *Land and the Politics of Belonging in Africa*, 21.

[53] See, for example, the argument of Mamdani, *Define and Rule: Native as Potential Reality*, 2.

[54] For further analysis concerning the rights of the indigenous peoples, see the analysis of E. Sjaastad and D.W. Bromley,

"Indigenous Land Rights in Sub-Saharan Africa: Appropriation, Security, and Investment Dynamics," *World Development* 25, 4 (June 1997): 549-562.

55 Mahmood Mamdani, "Can East African Federation go Beyond the Genocidal Concept of Tribal Homelands?" *http://in2eastafrica.net/can-east-african-federation-go-beyond-the-genocidal-concept-of-tribal-homelands?html* (Accessed January 2, 2014).

56 Ibid.

57 Stephen Castles and Alastair Davidson, *Citizenship and Migration: Globalization and the Politics of Belonging* (New York: Routledge, 2000), vii.

58 Ibid.

59 Stephen Castles and Alastair Davidson, *Citizenship and Migration: Globalization and the Politics of Belonging* (New York: Routledge, 2000), 32.

60 Benhabib, *The Rights of Others: Aliens, Residents, and Citizens* (Cambridge: Cambridge University Press, 2004), 120.

61 Castles and Davidson, *Citizenship and Migration: Globalization and the Politics of Belonging*, 11.

62 This condition is an impediment for the initiative of forming a strong East African Community. The leaders of the countries concerned have several times disagreed on the idea of entitling the citizens the right of land ownership anywhere within the region. Justifications given correlate to the argument that land cannot be given to foreigners. Citizens of these countries are also considered as citizens of the region, but each citizen can only own land in the country of birth.

63 Manby, *Struggles for Citizenship in Africa*, 160.

64 Abraham Korir Sing'Oei, "Citizenship in Kenya: The Nubian Case," in Brad K. Blitz and Maureen Lynch, eds.,

Statelessness and Citizenship: A Comparative Study on the Benefits Nationality (Northampton: Edward Elgar Publishing Limited, 2011), 45-65, at 57.

[65] Mahmood Mamdani, "African States, Citizenship, and War: A Case Study," *International Affairs* 78, 3 (August 2002): 493-506, at 505.

[66] Stephen Castles, "Globalization and the Ambiguities of National Citizenship," in Rainer Baubock and John Rundell, eds., *Blurred Boundaries: Migration, Ethnicity, Citizenship* (Aldershot: Ashgate, 1998), 223-244, at 228.

[67] Carens, "Aliens and Citizens: The Case for Open Borders," 221.

[68] Castles and Davidson, *Citizenship and Migration: Globalization and the Politics of Belonging*, xii.

Conclusion

The preceding evaluation provided a general picture surrounding land distribution, ownership, and management. We discovered that disputes emerge because of unequal distribution, mismanagement, lack of unified land law, and institutionalized corruption.The first chapter showed that claims of identity, belonging, and self-determination are limited because they tend to ignore the rights of others. A recourse to examine the link between land, morality, and market in the second chapter unveiled several weakness confirming the argument that the free market focuses on the interest of the minority with a possibility of undermining collective rights. The third chapter, from the perspective of migration, resettlement, and integration, revealed tendencies of marginalization and exclusiontoward migrants.

Arbitration of land-related disputes is difficult because one party of the claimants rely on statutory land rights system while the other rely on the customary land rights system. Experience shows that compromise is not forthcoming because land rights systems represent specific value systems accompanying ideologies of mutual exclusion. There cannot be a fair judgment because land rights systems function as competing value systems.

As a way of moving forwardwe have to identify the root causes of land disputes as we did in the discussion. Its relevance arises from the argument that African land rights systems must be studied with a view of trying to correct inherited inequalities from the past. Such a need cannot be ignored because the past is a part of us. It is a perspective that must be taken seriously because collective grievances are passed from one generation to anotherwith a possibility of obstructing any initiative geared toward reform. If past mistakes are not corrected, as a process of healing, they could linger on forever.

However, the initiative of going forwardshouldnot be limited to legal systems. The existing legal systems, most of which were inherited from colonial masters,are limited. The systemic weakness of the court systems arises from the fact that they are slow to reach decisions, intensify confusion, vulnerable to political manipulation, and underestimate the role of the African moral traditions. Legal approaches intensify confusion because they tend to lean more toward the tendency of applying outdated legal systems than creating systems that can address modern challenges.

Successful land reforms require effective methodologiesof implementing decisions we make. It is a process that requires dialogue as a means of bringing together parties concerned. On this account it is important to note that there are small-scale solutions that could be attained at the grassroots level. But permanent solutions, as our objective, will emerge from the process of establishing long-term structures ofgovernance.The process of building consensus must involve grassroots communities and participation of all institutions. This is an important aspect becauseland disputes touch the lives of all citizens. Varied experiences and contributions emerging from different institutions must be taken into account.

Problems that have made land reform initiatives ineffective include limited capability to implement agreed-upon resolutions, building institutions that can handle modern problems, formation of land commissions that can oversee the process of implementation, and inability to avoid politicization of land reforms. Addressing land disputes requires ability of balancing private and public interests.In this case, methodologies that seem to be effective include consensus-building, mutual-gain approach, and collaborative problem-solving. The weakness surrounding land commissions include the fact that they are unable to formulate methodologies that can enhance implementation as well as identify competent persons to take the responsibility of implementing the project. The task of implementation and management cannot be left to well-wishers, free market, or persons vying for political office.

Land reform programs can overcome poverty insofar as there is flexibility in the process of allocating land to people who need it to create wealth. This perspective entails surveying the land, formal documentation, and encouraging people to invest on land as a means of increasing production. In order to succeed we must move away from rigid legal standards and cultural traditions by adopting flexible possibilities that meet today's needs. We have to be practical in search for solutions that fit to the modern world, needs, and conditions of life. This perspective requires us to go beyond organizational regulations that obstruct reform and creativity. Governance must focus on performance rather than merely upholding tradition, uniformity, and authority. In this case the mindsets and attitudes of those administering land distribution and management must change.

One could argue that going beyond the disputes surrounding land rights systems entails getting rid of multiple land rights systems that maintain confusion. Rigid structures must be changed because they do not consider the condition of the poor, context, and accessibility. There is a need to create systems which are able to define responsibilities of the government and the landholder.It is important to know the problems surrounding the existing land rights systems, what we have to get rid of, what we want to achieve, and which methodologies of implementation are effective.

Looking into the future one can say that institutional reforms are indispensable.These reforms entail change of structures, policies, and ideologies that regulate public institutions. Regular evaluations are required because social conditions are always changing, and as such a change is required in order to be able to cope with the changes. A genuine reform must aim at building effective, transparent, and accountable public institutions intended to deliver public services to all citizens. These requirements are often ignored, and consequently many institutions become ineffective, outdated, and irrelevant. Institutional reform can be undertaken without foreign aid. Most of the civil servants believe that foreign aid is required for every public project. This way of thinking enslaves the mind because simple projects such as land survey, documentation of title deeds, and afforestation can easily be done without foreign assistance.

Land disputes can be averted as long as governance implement the following resolutions: first, modernization of land administration systems; second, decentralization of land registration systems; third, redistribution of land as a guarantee for shared growth; fourth, reformulation of methodologies of land planning, allocation, and management; fifth, increase land access for the vulnerable individuals, groups, and communities; sixth, promote community education on land registration, use, and management; seventh, improve land administration services by removing barriers of bureaucracy, corruption,and rigid policies in order to increase efficiency; eighth, modernize training of the land surveyors; ninth, generate effective methodologies of implementation; and tenth, overcome uncertainty over the role of the government.

Selected Bibliography

Ahrem, Kaj. The Maasai and the State: The Impact of Rural Development Policies on a Pastoral People in Tanzania. Copenhagen: International Work Group for Indigenous Affairs, 1995.

Akiwumi, A.M. Justice. "Report of the Judicial Commission Appointed to Inquire into Tribal Clashes in Kenya: Rift Valley." Daily Nation, Kenya (October 19, 2002): 12-26.

Akuffo, Kwame. "The Conception of Land Ownership in African Customary Law and Its Implication for Development." African Journal of International and Comparative Law 17, 1 (March 2009): 57-78.

Allan, A. John et al. Handbook of Land and Water Grabs in Africa: Foreign Direct Investment and Water Security. Oxford: Routledge, 2012.

Anseeuw, Ward and Alden Chris, eds. The Struggle Over Land in Africa: Conflicts, Politics, and Change. Cape Town: Human Sciences Research Council, 2010.

Bader, Veit et al. Citizenship and Exclusion. Hampshire: Macmillan Press, 1997.

Benhabib, Seyla. The Rights of Others: Aliens, Residents, and Citizens. Cambridge: Cambridge University Press, 2004.

Blitz, K. Brad and Lynch, Maureen, eds. Statelessness and Citizenship: A Comparative Study on the Benefits of Nationality. Northampton: Edward Elgar Publishing Limited, 2011.

Boos, Eric. "The Stratifying Effects of Globalization on Tanzanian Culture." Africa Tomorrow 2, 2 (June 2002): 119-145.

Busch, Lawrence. The Eclipse of Morality: Science, State, and Market. New York: Walter De Gruyter Inc., 2000.

Byamugisha, F.K. Frank, Securing Africa's Land for Shared Prosperity: A Program to Scale-Up Reforms and Investments. Washington, D.C.: World Bank, 2013.

Castles, Stephen and Davidson, Alistair. Citizenship and Migration: Globalization and the Politics of Belonging. New York: Rouledge, 2000.

Cernea, M. Michael and McDowell, Christopher, eds., Risks and Reconstruction: Experiences of Resettlers and Refugees. Washington, D.C.: World Bank, 2000.

Coughlin, M. Richard. Morality, Rationality, and Efficiency: New Perspectives on Socio-Economics. New York: M.E. Sharpe Inc., 1991.

Conrad, A. Christian. Morality and Economic Crisis: Enron, Subprime & Co. Hamburg: DiplomicaVerlag, 2010.

Collier, Paul. The Bottom Billion: Why the Poorest Countries are Failing and What Can be Done about It. Oxford: Oxford University Press, 2007.

Cotula, Lorenzo.The Great African Land Grab. London: Zed Books Limited, 2013.

Degeorges, Andre and Reilly, Brian. "Politicization of Land Reform in Zimbabwe: Impacts on Wildlife, Food Production, and the Economy." International Journal of Environmental Studies 64, 5 (October 2007): 571-586.

Derman, Bill et al., eds. Conflicts Over Land and Water in Africa. Oxford: Oxford University Press, 2007.

Downs, R.E. and Reyna, S.P., eds. Land and Society in Contemporary Africa. Hanover: University Press of New England, 1988.

Drobak, N. John and Nye, V.C. John, eds. The Frontiers of the New Institutional Economics. San Diego: Academic Press, 1907.

Dzislaw, Mach. Symbol, Conflict, and Identity: Essays in Political Anthropology. New York: State University of New York Press, 1993.

Dwyer, A. Judith, ed. The New Dictionary of Catholic Social Thought. Minnesota: The Liturgical Press, 1994.

George B.N. Ayittey, B.N. George. Indigenous African Institutions (New York: Transnational Publishers, 1991), 368.

GershonFeder and Raymond Noronha, "Land Rights Systems and Agricultural Development in Sub-Saharan Africa," Research Observer 2, 2 (July 1987): 143-169.

Githumo, waMwangi. Land and Nationalism. Washington, D.C.: University Press of America, 1981.

Gottlies, S. Roger, ed. The Sacred Earth: Religion, Nature, Environment (New York: Routledge, 1996).

Hart, John. The Spirit of Earth: A Theology of Land. New York: Paulist Press, 1984.

Holden, T. Stein et al., eds. The Emergence of Land Markets in Africa: Impacts on Poverty, Equity, and Efficiency. Washington, D.C.: Resources for the Future, 2009.

Hollenbach, David. "The Common Good Revisited." Theological Studies 50, 1 (March 1989): 70-94.

----------------------. Driven from Home: Protecting the Rights of Forced Migrants. Washington, D.C.: Georgetown University Press, 2010.

Houtart, Francois. Agrofuels: Big Profits, Ruined Lives and Ecological Destruction. Amsterdam: Pluto Press, 2010.

Kane, Abdoulaye and Leedy, H. Todd, eds. African Migrations: Patterns and Perspectives. Indiana: Indiana University Press, 2013.

Kanyinga, Karuti. Redistribution from Above: The Politics of Land Rights and Squatting on Coastal Kenya. Uppsala: NordiskaAfrikainstitutet, 2000.

Kenyatta, Jomo. Facing Mount Kenya. London: Vintage Books, 1938.

------------------. Suffering Without Bitterness. Nairobi: East African Publishing House, 1968.

Khamisi, Joseph. The Politics of Betrayal: Diary of the Kenyan Legislator. Trafford: Trafford Publishing, 2011.

Kiriswa, Benjamin. "African Model of Church as Family: Implications on Ministry and Leadership." AFER 43, 3 (June 2001): 99-108.

Klopp, M. Jacqueline. "Pilfering the Public: The Problem of Land Grabbing in Contemporary Kenya." Africa Today 47, 1 (Winter 2000): 7-26.

Kuba, Richard and Lentz, Carola eds. Land and the Politics of Belonging in West Africa. Leiden: Brill, 2006.

Leeming, A. David and Leeming, A. Margaret. A Dictionary of Creation Myths. Oxford: Oxford University Press, 2001.

Lemarchand, René. The Dynamics of Violence in Central Africa. Philadelphia: Pennsylvania University Press, 2009.

Locke, John. Two Treatises of Government. New York: Hafner Publishing Company, 1947.

Long, Norman. Family and Work in Rural Societies: Perspectives on Non-Wage Labor. London: Tavistock Publications, 1984.

Lukudu, Ceasar et al. Alienation of Public Land in Kenya. Nairobi: Catholic University of Eastern Africa, 2000.

Lund, Christian. Land Rights and Citizenship in Africa. Uppsala: NordiskaAfrikainstitutet, 2011.

Mamdani, Mahmood. Scholars in the Marketplace: The Dilemmas of Neo-Liberal Reform at Makerere. Kampala: Fountain Publishers, 2007.

-------------------------. Define and Rule: Native as Political Reality. Cambridge: Harvard University Press, 2012.

-----------------------. "African States, Citizenship, and War: A Case Study," International Affairs 78, 3 (August 2002): 493-506.

Manji, S. Ambreena. The Politics of Land Reform in Africa: From Communal Tenure to Free Markets. London: Zed Books, 2006.

Manby, Browen. Struggles for Citizenship in Africa. London: Zed Books, 2009.

Matondi, B. Prosper et al., eds. Biofuels, Land Grabbing, and Food Security in Africa. London: Zed Books Limited, 2011.

Menzel, C. Donald. Ethics of Management for Public Administrators: Building Organizations of Integrity. New York: M.E. Sharpe, 2000.

Milbank, John. Theology and Social Theory: Beyond Secular Reason. Cambridge: Blackwell Publishers, 1993.

Minow, Martha. Between Vengeance and Forgiveness: Facing History after Genocide and Mass Violence. Boston: Beacon Press, 1998.

Montesquieu, de Baron. The Spirit of the Laws, trans. Anne Cohler, Basia Miller, and Harold Stone, Cambridge: Cambridge University Press, 1989.

Moyo, Sam. African Land Question, Agrarian Transactions and the State: Contradictions of Neo-Liberal Land Reform. Dakar: Sapes Books, 2008.

Mufune, Pempelani. "Land Reform Management in Namibia, South Africa, and Zimbabwe: A Comparative Perspective." International Journal of Rural Management 6, 1 (June 2010): 1-31.

Naessen A. Van et al., eds. The Diversity of Development: Essays in Honor of Jan Kleinpenning (Assen: Van Gorcum, 1997).

Ndungu Report. "Land Graft in Kenya." Review of African Political Economy 32, 103 (March 2005): 142-151.

Nmah, E. Patrick. "Spiritual Dimension of Land Identity Crisis in Igboland of Nigeria."Unizik Journal of Arts and Humanities 12, 2 (January 2011): 136-151.

Nyerere, Julius. "Ujamaa: The Basis of African Socialism." The Journal of Pan African Studies 1, 1 (June 1987): 4-11.

Okuku, Anthony Juma. "Civil Society and Democratization Processes in Kenya and Uganda: A Comparative Analysis of the Contribution of the Church and NGOs." South African Journal of Political Studies 30, 1 (May 2003): 51-63.

Palmer, Robin. "The Land Problems in Africa: The Second Scramble." New People 54 (June 2002): 13-22.

Peters, E. Pauline. "Inequality and Social Conflict Over Land in Africa," Journal of Agrarian Change 4, 3 (June 2004): 269-314.

Pogee, Thomas and Mollendorf, Darrel, eds. Global Justice: Seminal Essays. Minnesota: Paragon House, 2008.

Plateau, Jean-Philippe. Land Reform and Structural Adjustment in Sub-Saharan Africa: Controversies and

Guidelines. Rome: Food and Agricultural Organization, Economic and Social Policy Department, 1992.

Polanyi, Karl. The Great Transformation. Boston: Beacon Press, 1957.

Powelson, John. The Moral Economy. Michigan: University of Michigan Press, 1998.

Quan, Julian et al., eds. Land in Africa: Market Asset or Secure Livelihood. London: Royal African Society, 2004.

Sandel, J. Michael. What Money Can't Buy: The Moral Limits of Markets. New York: Farrah, Straus, and Giroux, 2012.

Sen, Amartya. On Ethics and Economics. Oxford: Blackwell Publishers, 1987.

Sinha, Radha. Landlessness: A Growing Problem. Rome: Food and Agriculture Organization of the United Nations, 1994.

Sirico, A. Robert. Defending Free Market: The Moral Case for a Free Economy. Massachusetts: Regnery Publishing Inc., 2012.

Soto, De Hernando. The Mystery of Capital: Why Capitalism Triumphs in the West and Fails Everywhere Else. New York: Basic Books, 2000.

Schutter, De Olivier. "How Not to Think of Land-Grabbing: Three Critiques of Large-Scale Investments in Farmland." Journal of Peasant Studies 38, 2 (March 2011): 249-279.

Shipton, Parker. Mortgaging the Ancestors: Ideologies of Attachment in Africa. New Haven: Yale University Press, 2009.

Toulmin, Camila and Quan, Julian Quan, eds. Evolving Land Rights, Policy and Tenure in Africa. London: IIED, 2000.

United Nations, Habitat. "World Urban Forum: Cities without Slums." United Nations Habitat (May 2000): 1-15.

Urmilla, Bob. "Land-Related Conflicts in Sub-Saharan Africa." African Journal of Conflict Resolution 10, 2 (June 2010): 49-64.

Wanjala C. Smokin. Land Law and Disputes in Kenya. Nairobi: Oxford University Press, 1990.

Warioba, Joseph. "The Report of the Warioba Commission on Corruption." Business Times Supplement (June 27, 1997): 1-33.

Weber, Max. The Protestant Ethic and the Spirit of Capitalism, trans. by Talcott Persons. New York: Dover Publications Inc., 2003.

Wogaman, Philip. Economics and Ethics. Philadelphia: Fortress Press, 1986.

World Council of Churches. Land Rights for Indigenous People. Geneva: World Council of Churches, 1983.

Wrong, Michela. It's Our Turn to Eat: The Story of Kenyan Whistle-Blower. New York: Harper Collins, 2009.

www.ingramcontent.com/pod-product-compliance
Lightning Source LLC
Chambersburg PA
CBHW032351280326
41935CB00008B/537